PROFESSIONAL
RESOURCES

Making and Writing Words

Grades 3-6

by
Timothy Rasinski, Ph.D.

Editor
Hank Rudisill

Cover Design
Julie Webb

The art of teaching is the art of assisting discovery.

—Mark Van Doren

The knowledge of words is the gate to scholarship.

—Woodrow Wilson

ISBN 0-88724-560-9

Table of Contents

Why Making and Writing Words? 4

How To Use This Book 6

Generic Worksheet 11

References 158

Notes 159

Making and Writing Words Lessons

golden 12

market 14

awesome 16

chimney.................... 18

courage.................... 20

cyclone 22

dessert 24

freedom 26

kitchen 28

machine.................... 30

private 32

alphabet 34

aluminum 36

astonish 38

barnyard 40

carnival.................... 42

champion 44

creature 46

cupboard 48

daydream 50

elevator..................... 52

enormous 54

festival...................... 56

guardian 58

magician................... 60

marathon 62

nuisance 64

ordinary.................... 66

pamphlet 68

parakeet 70

pleasure 72

reporter.................... 74

sandwich 76

sculpture................... 78

skeleton 80

stranger 82

sympathy.................. 84

violence 86

yearbook................... 88

apologize.................. 90

architect 92

cooperate.................. 94

delicious................... 96

equipment 98

exhibitor 100

furniture 102

guarantee................. 104

hurricane 106

satellite.................... 108

southwest 110

technique................. 112

telephone................. 114

telescope 116

volunteer 118

hemisphere 120

predator 122

theaters 124

adventure................. 126

advertise 128

astounded 130

frostbite 132

periscope 134

residence 136

spectator 138

temporary 140

confidence 142

experiment 144

impossible 146

starvation................ 148

suggestion 150

celebration 152

independent............. 154

masterpiece 156

Why Making and Writing Words?

Reading is a complex phenomenon. It is a cognitive act. It is a physical act. It involves our emotional and social selves. How we read and how we learn to read is still a matter of study by scholars around the world.

Despite the enormous complexity of reading, one of the most critical parts of the reading process is decoding or identifying words. In many ways, word identification—going from the written to the oral form of words—is a defining feature of reading. For many children, trouble with word identification is what makes reading difficult. Whether taught using a highly intensive phonics approach or a whole language approach, all children need practice in word identification. Reading scholars, curriculum and instruction specialists, and teachers are constantly searching for instructional methods to help children efficiently learn to identify words in print.

In 1992, a professional article by Patricia and James Cunningham appeared in *The Reading Teacher*. The article was entitled "Making Words: Enhancing the Invented Spelling-Decoding Connection" and described an approach to the teaching of word recognition (decoding) and its complement, spelling (encoding), in classrooms. The simplicity of the activity and its instructional elegance were striking. In the Cunninghams' activity, students worked under the guidance of their teacher in "Making Words." Students manipulated a limited set of letter cards to make a series of words, beginning with short words and working their way to longer, more complex words. The fast-paced activity required only minutes to complete. Yet those few minutes were filled with high-level problem solving and word exploration. Done regularly, this activity can help students to make significant gains in learning to read.

Leading literacy scholars have noted the potential of Making Words as a way to promote word learning. In a study of approaches for teaching phonics and word recognition that appeared in *Reading Research Quarterly*, Stahl, Duffy-Hester, and Stahl (1998) wrote that "Making Words" appears to be "effective as part of (an) overall approach to teaching reading" (p. 347). Making Words was also described as "an engaging medium for explicit instruction about specific spelling-sound correspondences and the alphabetic principle" (p. 198) in the book *Preventing Reading Difficulties in Young Children* (Snow, Burns, & Griffin, 1998).

A Balanced Reading Program—The Four-Blocks™ Model

Making Words is one part of a larger, balanced reading program. Balanced programs strive to integrate the best features of holistic, whole language literacy and skill-oriented, direct instruction reading programs. These reading and writing activities are balanced with instruction in the skills and strategies related to reading, such as decoding, learning to spell, and learning the meaning of words. Without the ability to decode quickly, fluently, and automatically, as well as the ability to understand the meaning of words, students' reading comprehension is likely to suffer. Although opportunities for students to learn words is part of a balanced literacy approach, it is only one part of a larger curricular framework that allows students to put their word learning to use in real reading and writing situations.

The Making Words activity is a key element in the Working with Words block of the Four-Blocks™ Literacy Model (a balanced literacy approach by Patricia Cunningham and Dorothy Hall in which the reading and writing curriculum is divided into four fairly equal time blocks—a block for independent reading called Self-Selected Reading, a block for in-depth reading called Guided Reading, the Writing block, and a block for word study called Working with Words). In Making Words, students regularly have opportunities to make words under the guidance of their teacher. Other word study activities also take place during the time allotted, but the Making Words activity is at the foundation of the Working with Words block.

This text focuses on Making and Writing Words, a version of the original Making Words activity that has been adapted for older students (third grade and above) who have developed some proficiency in writing. Instead of using letter cards, *Making and Writing Words* uses a blank worksheet. Students actually write down the words as they are guided through the activity. The physical act of writing the words helps to reinforce the students' memories of the words.

Making and Writing Words is an excellent vehicle for teaching spelling and word recognition. Used regularly, students can develop a firm understanding of how words are decoded and spelled—in short, how words work! With this book as a resource, planning a Making and Writing Words lesson is easy, and implementing the activity is quick. The level of engagement on the part of the students is high, and even though only a small amount of time is invested in the activity, the results reflect a lot of learning. If Making and Writing Words is done regularly (3-4 times per week throughout the school year), normally-developing students as well as those students who are struggling in word recognition and decoding will make great strides in their ability to decode and spell the words they encounter in their reading and the words they use in their writing.

How To Use This Book

This book provides you with all you need to implement 73 Making and Writing Words lessons. Each lesson is followed by the corresponding student worksheet. You simply need to make a copy for each student as well as a transparency for yourself. Each of the Making and Writing Words lessons contains the consonants and vowels that make up the challenge word and the other words to be made with these letters, including clues in the form of sentences. Also included are transfer words and suggested sorting activities.

First, you will need to decide which worksheet—the generic worksheet or the worksheet designed for each lesson—you would like to use for each lesson. A generic worksheet that can be used for any lesson has been provided (see page 11). This worksheet provides boxes for the initial writing of letters, an ordered list of boxes for Making and Writing Words, and a set of boxes for making and writing the transfer words. This worksheet can also be used for any lessons you may wish to develop on your own or lessons from other sources.

In addition, this book also includes a worksheet for each specific lesson. The worksheet can provide extra help for students in mapping letters onto individual sounds. In these worksheets, the word boxes are further divided into letter boxes to provide students with information about the number of letters in each word. Vowels are marked by gray shaded boxes (see example below). Although *y* can sometimes be used as a vowel, for the purposes of this book, *y* will always be listed in the consonants box at the top of the teacher's page. If *y* may be used as a vowel in the lesson, it will be listed with an asterisk (y*). Letter boxes for *y* will not be shaded, even if it is used as a vowel in the word (see example below). It is up to you to decide if and how you want to explain the treatment of *y* as a vowel to your students. As an additional part of the activity, you may wish to have students use their pencils to shade in the boxes where *y* is used as a vowel.

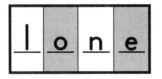   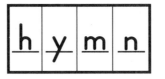

If you choose to implement a lesson using the worksheet with the letter boxes, follow the exact order provided in the lesson plan. These worksheets are designed to go with each lesson. If you choose to go with the generic worksheet, you may take liberties with the order of the words or add or delete any words in a given lesson.

Listed on the next page are the steps you will need to follow to implement a *Making and Writing Words* lesson successfully.

Before the Lesson:

Choose the lesson and the worksheet you wish to use and make a copy of the blank worksheet for each student. Then, make an overhead transparency of the form so you can guide students in Making and Writing Words while they complete the activity on their own worksheets.

Beginning the Making and Writing Words Lesson:

1. Distribute copies of the *Making and Writing Words* worksheet to students, asking them to work with pencils since they may wish to make changes to the words they write.
2. Have students write the vowels and consonants to be used in the lesson in the appropriate boxes at the top of the worksheet.
3. Tell students you will pronounce words for them and give them a sentence clue.
4. Students should write the words in the appropriate boxes using only the letters at the top of the worksheet. Remind students they will cut out the words later in the activity, so they need to make their letters fit within the boxes. Allow students to work with partners or to talk with a partner if they have problems with any word they will be making. (Many students seem to learn best when they work this way.) Indicate that you will also be writing the words on the transparency, so if students want to check their answers or need extra help, they can refer to it.
5. Note that you will be beginning with short words and gradually progressing to longer words. Your presentation of words to students may include one or more of the following approaches:
   • Pronouncing the word
   • Telling the number of letters in the word (useful when using the generic worksheet)
6. When you get to the challenge (15th) word, tell students only that the final word uses all the letters. Students love the challenge of figuring out this mystery word!

(See the example of a completed student lesson sheet on page 10.)

Continuing the Making and Writing Words Lesson

Word Sorts:

The next portion of the lesson is the word sorts. Students can cut out the words they have just written into individual word cards, or you can write and sort the words on the overhead projector or the chalkboard with the class. (If you choose to have students cut out the words and want them to keep their original, completed *Making and Writing Words* worksheets, you will need to make copies of their completed worksheets before beginning the word sorts. You can also write the words on the generic form on page 11 and make a copy for each student to cut out and sort.) Once the word cards are cut out, students can complete a variety of word card/word bank activities including word sorts, word games, alphabetizing, and simple word practice with a partner. Give students envelopes in which to store their word cards.

- To do word sorts with students, begin with the suggestions given with each lesson. Tell students the categories and ask them to sort the words into those categories. You may have students sort by categories based on the presence or absence of a particular word feature (words with consonant blends and words with no consonant blends; words with long vowel sounds, words with no long vowel sounds, etc.). Or, you may have students sort by multiple categories (sort the words into three piles—those with one syllable, those with two syllables, and those with three or more syllables). Over the course of a day or two, you can lead students through several sorts.

- Encourage students to sort the words into those that have other words within them, and those that do not have other words within them. For example, the word *one* can be found within the word *phone*. A very productive strategy for decoding (and understanding) unfamiliar words is to examine the unknown word for familiar words or letter patterns.

- As students become more adept at sorting and categorizing, you may ask them to come up with their own categories for the word sorts.

- One of the more challenging forms of word sorts is called an open word sort. In this version of word sorting, you (or one of the students if students are working in pairs) begin to sort the words into piles without telling the students (or partner) what those piles represent. The students' (or partner's) job is to figure out the categories by observing the way in which the words are sorted.

Word sorts work because they encourage students to look at the given words multiple times. However, rather than simply looking at each word in the same way each time, students must analyze the words from a different perspective with each sort—one time by the presence or absence of a consonant blend, the next time by the presence or absence of a particular word family, vowel sound, or number of syllables per word, etc. These multiple analyses give students the opportunity to make in-depth examinations of the words and develop greater control and understanding over the given words and the various word features used as categories.

Transfer:

The final part of the lesson is the transfer portion. Here, students use the letter and sound knowledge from the first part of the lesson and combine it with other letters that are not part of the lesson to form new words. Possible transfer words are presented with each lesson plan. The transfer portion of the lesson can take place immediately after the initial Making and Writing Words activity, or it can occur sometime shortly thereafter.

Extension Ideas:

If you use the letter box worksheet for a particular lesson, you may wish to follow up by using the generic form for the same lesson at a later date. The generic form requires students to infer more about the words.

The high-frequency words used in any of these lessons can eventually find their way onto your classroom word wall where students can continue practicing the words and using the words in their oral and written language. Some of the words from a *Making and Writing Words* lesson can also be employed as weekly spelling words for students.

Sample of a completed student lesson sheet prior to sorting:

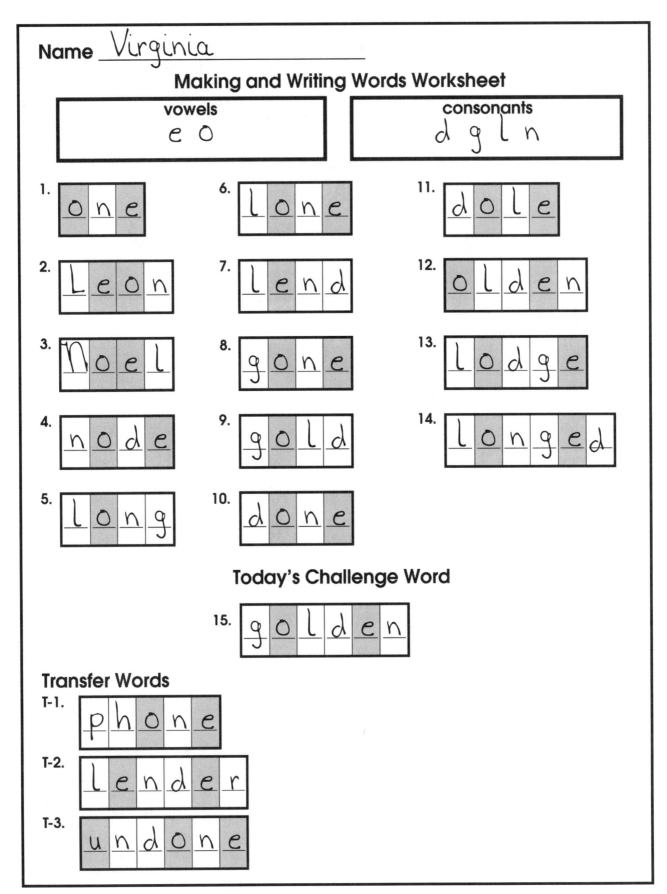

Name __Virginia__

Making and Writing Words Worksheet

vowels	consonants
e o	d g l n

1. o n e

6. l o n e

11. d o l e

2. L e o n

7. l e n d

12. o l d e n

3. N o e l

8. g o n e

13. l o d g e

4. n o d e

9. g o l d

14. l o n g e d

5. l o n g

10. d o n e

Today's Challenge Word

15. g o l d e n

Transfer Words

T-1. p h o n e

T-2. l e n d e r

T-3. u n d o n e

10

Name _____

Making and Writing Words Worksheet

vowels	consonants

1.	6.	11.
2.	7.	12.
3.	8.	13.
4.	9.	14.
5.	10.	15.

T-1.	T-2.	T-3.

Making and Writing Words Lesson
Challenge Word: golden

vowels	consonants
e, o	**d, g, l, n**

Making Words

	Words	Sentence Clue
1.	one	*The Wizard of Oz* is one of my favorite movies.
2.	Leon	My best friend is Leon Smith.
3.	Noel	My favorite Christmas carol is *The First Noel*.
4.	node	After I fell, my elbow swelled into a large node.
5.	long	It is a long time until summer vacation.
6.	lone	The pilot was the lone survivor of the airplane crash.
7.	lend	Could you please lend me a dollar for lunch today?
8.	gone	He was gone in a flash!
9.	gold	Gold and silver are expensive metals.
10.	done	Our work was done within an hour.
11.	dole	Mom promised to dole out my allowance this week.
12.	olden	In olden days, children did not receive allowances.
13.	lodge	We stayed at the lodge when we went on the ski trip.
14.	longed	My brother longed for his friend when she moved away.
15.	golden	

Sorts:

1 or 2 syllable words; words containing long vowel sounds; words containing silent letters; words containing consonant blends

Transfer Words

	Words	Clue
1.	phone	Mom used her mobile phone to report the accident.
2.	lender	The local bank is a major lender of money.
3.	undone	In most fairy tales, the witch's spell is eventually undone.

Name _____

Making and Writing Words Worksheet

vowels	consonants

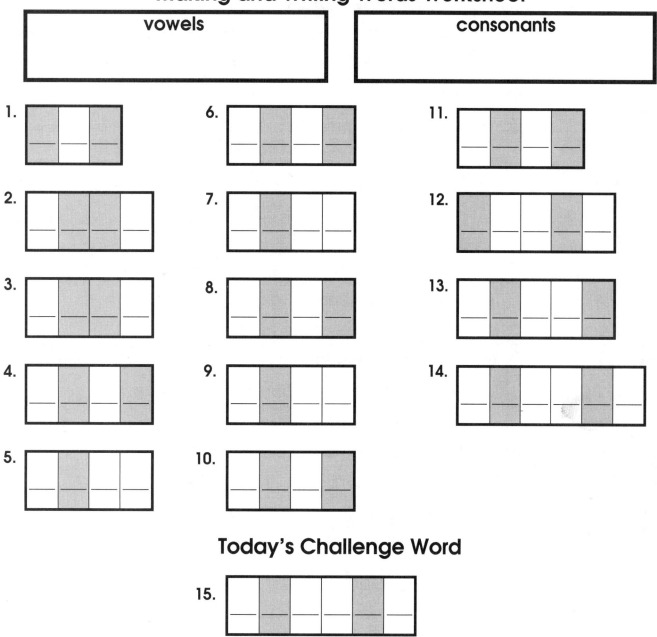

1.

6.

11.

2.

7.

12.

3.

8.

13.

4.

9.

14.

5.

10.

Today's Challenge Word

15.

Transfer Words

T-1.

T-2.

T-3.

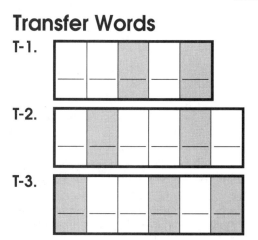

13

Making and Writing Words Lesson
Challenge Word: market

vowels	consonants
a, e	**k, m, r, t**

Making Words

	Words	Sentence Clue
1.	tear	A tear ran down from the child's eye.
2.	trek	It is a long trek across Alaska.
3.	term	I wonder if the president will run for a second term.
4.	rate	My dad received a raise in his pay rate.
5.	rake	Every fall, my parents rake the leaves in our yard.
6.	meat	Hamburger is my favorite kind of meat.
7.	mate	The first mate gave the captain's orders to the sailors.
8.	mart	My parents like to shop at the local food mart.
9.	mark	I made a mark on the sidewalk with chalk.
10.	mare	A female horse is called a mare.
11.	make	How long did it take you to make that sculpture?
12.	tamer	I think our dog is tamer than your cat.
13.	taker	I could not find a taker for my bicycle at the yard sale.
14.	maker	A cobbler is a maker of shoes and boots.
15.	market	

Sorts:
words containing the long "a" sound; words containing the "er" sound; words that refer to living things

Transfer Words

	Words	Clue
1.	marker	That permanent marker will not wash out of your clothes.
2.	inmate	He was an inmate in the county jail for six months.
3.	termite	The termite inspector comes to our home once a year.

Name _____

Making and Writing Words Worksheet

vowels	consonants

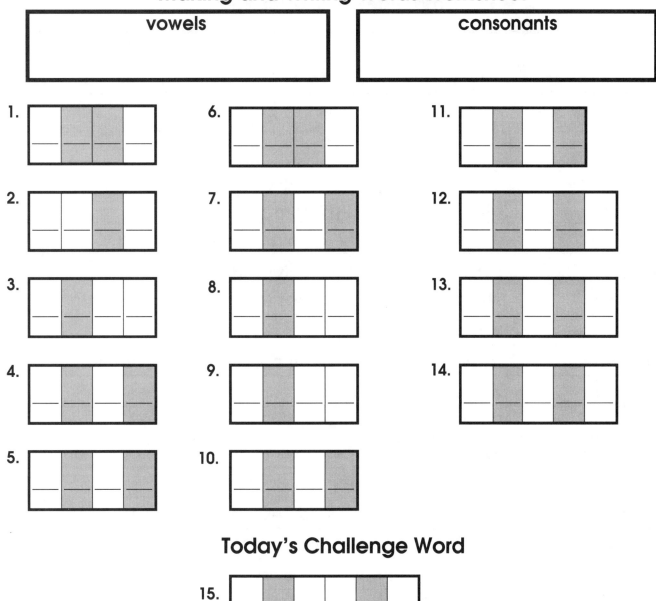

1.
2.
3.
4.
5.
6.
7.
8.
9.
10.
11.
12.
13.
14.

Today's Challenge Word

15.

Transfer Words

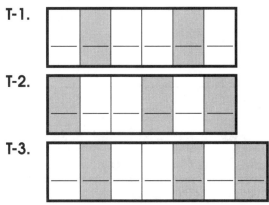

T-1.

T-2.

T-3.

Making and Writing Words Lesson
Challenge Word: awesome

vowels	consonants
a, e, e, o	**m, s, w**

Making Words

Words	Sentence Clue
1. see	I can barely see in this fog.
2. saw	I saw your books on top of your desk.
3. mow	I mow the yard when the grass gets too long.
4. awe	I am in awe of my big sister's track records.
5. woes	My dog sang out his woes to the full moon last night.
6. swam	Lisa swam across the pool to meet Mike.
7. some	I have some stickers, but not as many as Jenny.
8. seem	We seem to like the same things.
9. seam	The seam in his pants split when he fell down.
10. same	Amy and I have the same white shirt with black buttons.
11. owes	My brother owes me ten dollars.
12. mesa	The village was located near the edge of the mesa.
13. meow	My cat will purr and meow when you pet her.
14. ease	The bandage helped to ease my hurt elbow.
15. awesome	

Sorts:
1 and 2 syllable words; words containing long "o" sounds; words containing long "e" sounds; words that show action (verbs)

Transfer Words

Words	Clue
1. sane	It is important to act sane and responsible in a museum.
2. easy	The new game is easy to learn and fun to play.
3. seamless	The dress my mother made was nearly seamless.

Name _____

Making and Writing Words Worksheet

vowels	consonants

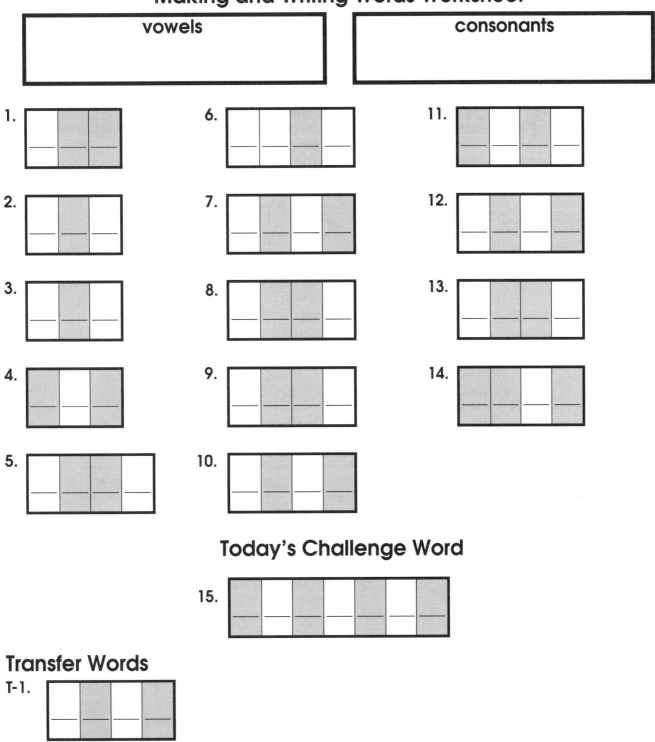

1.

2.

3.

4.

5.

6.

7.

8.

9.

10.

11.

12.

13.

14.

Today's Challenge Word

15.

Transfer Words

T-1.

T-2.

T-3.

17

Making and Writing Words Lesson
Challenge Word: chimney

vowels **e, i**	consonants **c, h, m, n, y***

Making Words

Words	Sentence Clue
1. ice	I always put ice in my soda pop.
2. icy	The water in the lake was icy and cold.
3. him	I will go to the store with him.
4. hen	The hen on the farm laid five eggs last week.
5. hem	My mom had to hem the bottom of my skirt.
6. men	The men worked to restore power after the storm.
7. nice	The dog next door is very nice to me.
8. mine	The book is mine, but the notebook is Henry's.
9. mice	The mice were caught in the new traps we bought.
10. inch	I grew more than an inch over the summer.
11. hymn	We sang a hymn during the service yesterday.
12. chin	I have a scratch on my chin.
13. mince	My mother doesn't mince words when she gets angry.
14. chime	The wind chime makes a beautiful sound.
15. chimney	

Sorts:

words containing long "i" sounds; words containing short "i" sounds; words containing a silent "e"; words naming or describing living things

Transfer Words

Words	Clue
1. hymnal	I found the song in the church hymnal.
2. mining	Grandfather lived in a coal mining town in West Virginia.
3. shine	Mike polished the table to a brilliant, glossy shine.

Name _____

Making and Writing Words Worksheet

vowels	consonants

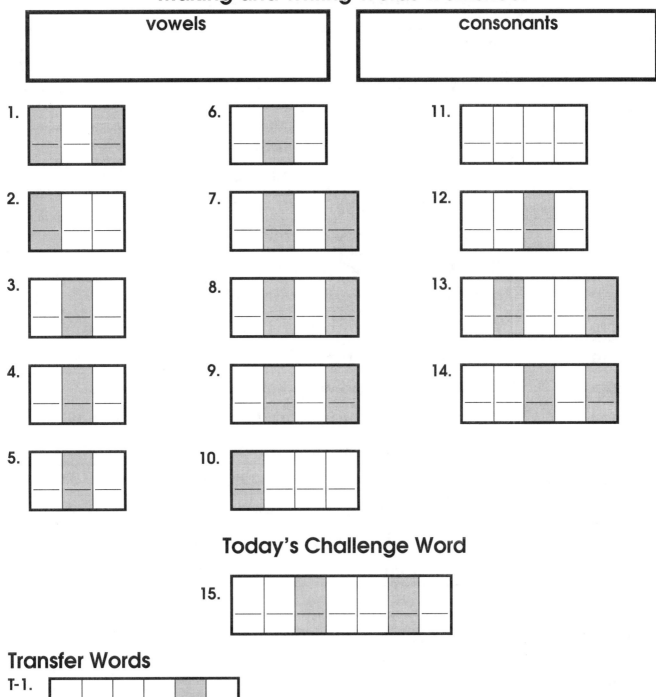

1.

6.

11.

2.

7.

12.

3.

8.

13.

4.

9.

14.

5.

10.

Today's Challenge Word

15.

Transfer Words

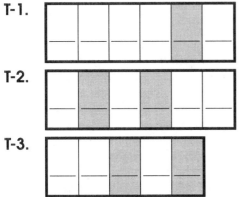

T-1.

T-2.

T-3.

Making and Writing Words Lesson
Challenge Word: courage

vowels	consonants
a, e, o, u	**c, g, r**

Making Words

	Words	Sentence Clue
1.	race	I ran the race and won first prize.
2.	urge	Last night I had an urge to eat pizza.
3.	gear	I broke the gear shift on my bicycle.
4.	gore	The war movie had plenty of blood and gore in it.
5.	cure	I hope we find a cure for cancer soon.
6.	core	When I finished my apple, I threw away the core.
7.	care	I take very good care of my dog, Ginger.
8.	cage	The lions in the zoo were kept in a large cage.
9.	rage	The rage of the lions showed that they hated captivity.
10.	acre	My parents own one acre of land.
11.	grace	The swans swam with grace and elegance on the lake.
12.	cargo	The cargo plane carried supplies to the settlement.
13.	argue	The boys in our class yell and argue a lot.
14.	cougar	I was frightened by the cougar at the zoo.
15.	courage	

Sorts:

1 and 2 syllable words; words containing long "a" sounds; words containing silent letters

Transfer Words

	Words	Clue
1.	graceful	A ballerina is a very graceful dancer.
2.	enrage	Don't enrage Father while he is on the phone.
3.	stage	We set up the stage to look like an enchanted forest.

Name _____

Making and Writing Words Worksheet

vowels	consonants

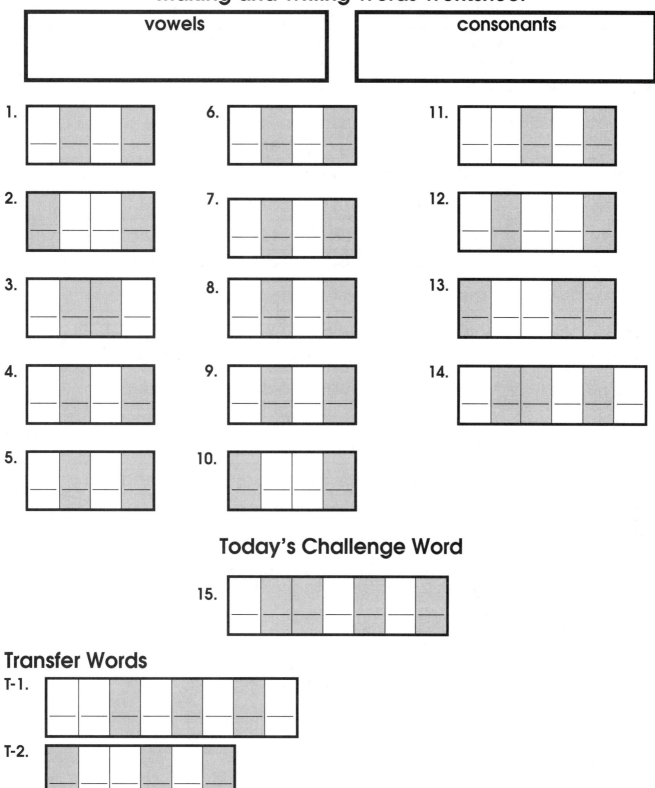

1.

2.

3.

4.

5.

6.

7.

8.

9.

10.

11.

12.

13.

14.

Today's Challenge Word

15.

Transfer Words

T-1.

T-2.

T-3.

Making and Writing Words Lesson
Challenge Word: cyclone

vowels
e, o

consonants
c, c, l, n, y*

Making Words

	Words	Sentence Clue
1.	on	The cup is sitting on top of the table in the kitchen.
2.	one	I have only one hat to wear outside.
3.	yen	The Japanese equivalent to the dollar is called the yen.
4.	coy	My brother tends to act very coy around adults.
5.	eon	It takes one billion years to make an eon.
6.	only	I only have enough money to buy a sandwich for lunch.
7.	once	I once found a four leaf clover in our yard.
8.	Noel	My best friend's name is Noel Johnson.
9.	Cole	*Old King Cole* is one of my favorite nursery rhymes.
10.	lone	The lone wolf howled in the moonlight.
11.	cone	I would prefer to get two scoops of ice cream in a cone.
12.	cycle	There are several stages in the life cycle of a butterfly.
13.	Coney	Coney Island is a large amusement park.
14.	clone	Scientists successfully made a clone of a sheep.
15.	cyclone	

Sorts:

1, 2, and 3 syllable words; words containing long "e" sounds; words containing long "o" sounds; words that denote singularity

Transfer Words

	Words	Clue
1.	lonely	James felt lonely when his sister went away to school.
2.	loneliest	I am always loneliest when I am home alone at night.
3.	bicycle	Ann rode her bicycle to her best friend's house.

Name _____

Making and Writing Words Worksheet

vowels	consonants

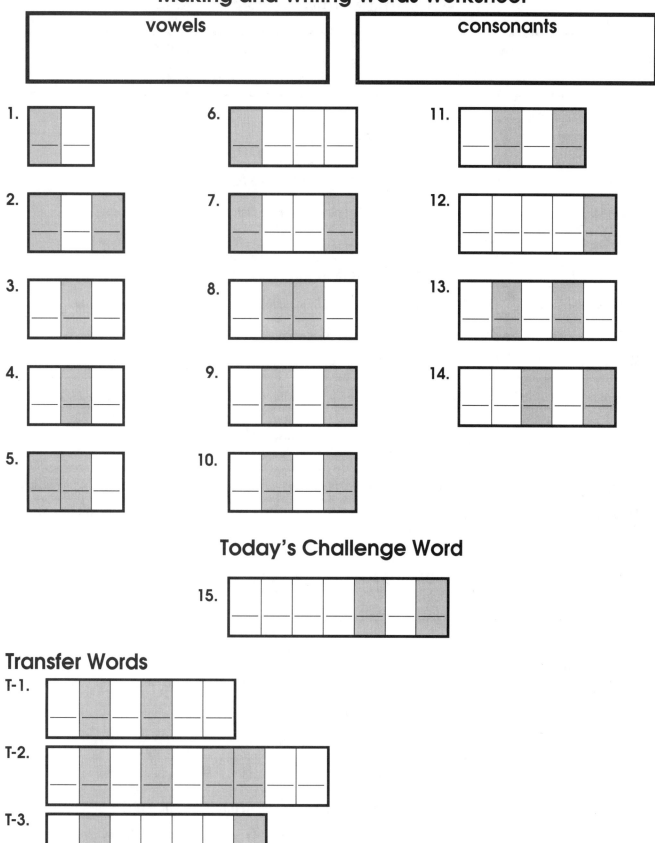

1.

2.

3.

4.

5.

6.

7.

8.

9.

10.

11.

12.

13.

14.

Today's Challenge Word

15.

Transfer Words

T-1.

T-2.

T-3.

23

Making and Writing Words Lesson
Challenge Word: dessert

vowels	consonants
e, e	**d, r, s, s, t**

Making Words

	Words	Sentence Clue
1.	sets	Emily has three sets of water color paints.
2.	sees	Our teacher sees us every day in the classroom.
3.	Tess	Tess Harper is an actress whom I admire.
4.	rest	When I am very tired, I sit down and rest.
5.	deer	I saw three deer while walking through the woods.
6.	trees	The trees in the woods are very tall and spindly.
7.	steed	The knight and his steed were dressed in shining armor.
8.	seeds	Mrs. Denson planted some carrot seeds in her garden.
9.	reeds	Where are the reeds for the clarinets?
10.	dress	My blue dress is long and elegant.
11.	steer	The sailor was told to steer the ship away from the rocks.
12.	rested	Once he was rested, the dog ran around the yard again.
13.	deters	The angry dog deters me from going into his yard.
14.	deserts	The deserts of Africa are very large and dry.
15.	dessert	

Sorts:
words referring to living things; words containing long "e" sounds; words containing "er" sounds; words containing suffixes or inflected endings; words with double letters

Transfer Words

	Words	Clue
1.	seedling	We planted an oak seedling this spring.
2.	seeding	Mother is seeding her garden with a variety of flowers.
3.	dressing	I like to put Italian dressing on my salad.

Name _____

Making and Writing Words Worksheet

vowels	consonants

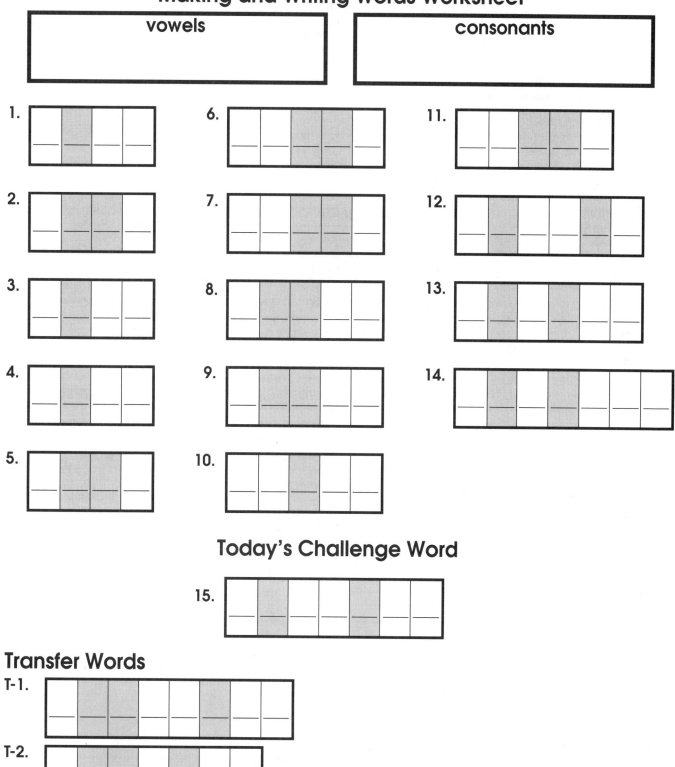

1.

6.

11.

2.

7.

12.

3.

8.

13.

4.

9.

14.

5.

10.

Today's Challenge Word

15.

Transfer Words

T-1.

T-2.

T-3.

25

© Carson-Dellosa CD-2600

Making and Writing Words Lesson
Challenge Word: freedom

vowels	consonants
e, e, o	**d, f, m, r**

Making Words

	Words	Sentence Clue
1.	rode	I rode the horses at my uncle's ranch.
2.	more	The more I see my grandmother, the more I love her.
3.	from	The new students are from the other side of town.
4.	fore	The golfer yelled, "Fore!" as his golf ball flew our way.
5.	form	You must have good form and posture to be a ballerina.
6.	feed	During the winter, I like to feed hungry birds.
7.	dorm	My brother lives in a dorm room at college.
8.	dome	The dome of the Capitol building is very impressive.
9.	deer	While at camp, we sometimes see deer in the woods.
10.	freed	Many slaves were freed by the Underground Railroad.
11.	erode	The barren hilltop is beginning to erode.
12.	defer	I usually defer to my parents on important questions.
13.	deform	I can deform my basketball by standing on it.
14.	formed	I formed a snowman out of the new fallen snow.
15.	freedom	

Sorts:
words containing long "e" sounds; words containing "or" sounds; words referring to places or things

Transfer Words

	Words	Clue
1.	before	Before I can play, I have to clean up my bedroom.
2.	formal	You should wear formal clothes on special occasions.
3.	dormitory	When you go to college, you may live in a dormitory.

Name _____

Making and Writing Words Worksheet

vowels	consonants

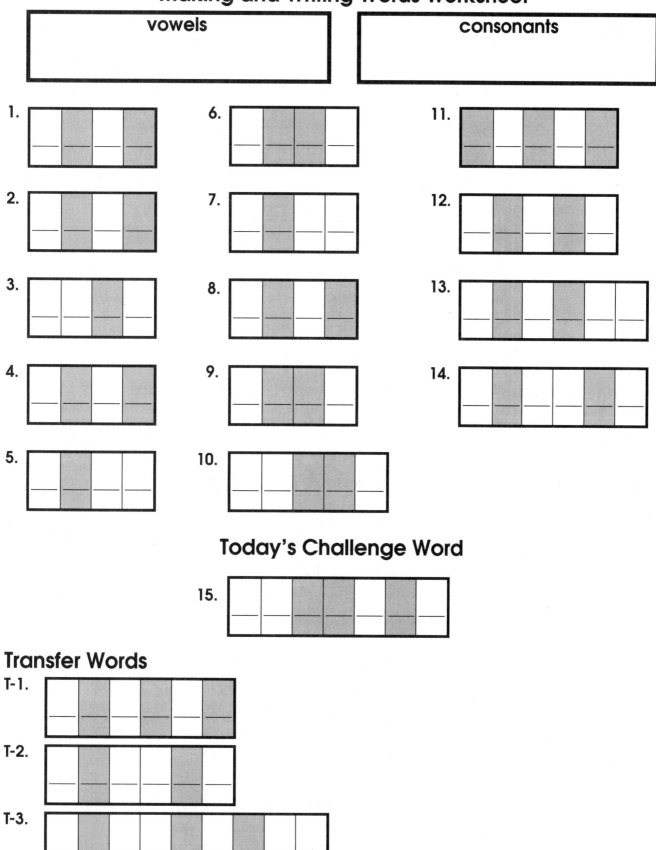

Today's Challenge Word

15.

Transfer Words

T-1.

T-2.

T-3.

27

Making and Writing Words Lesson
Challenge Word: kitchen

vowels	consonants
e, i	**c, h, k, n, t**

Making Words

	Words	Sentence Clue
1.	knit	My grandma is teaching me how to knit.
2.	kite	I flew my kite in the park.
3.	itch	When I have an itch, I just have to scratch it.
4.	inch	A ruler is a good instrument to measure one inch.
5.	hint	Mr. Hill gave me a hint to help me answer the question.
6.	thin	One piece of paper is very thin.
7.	then	First I will eat dinner, then I will brush my teeth.
8.	etch	With Mom's help, I will etch a picture on the glass cup.
9.	chin	My dad grew a beard on his chin.
10.	cent	A penny is worth one cent.
11.	thick	That tree trunk is very thick and sturdy.
12.	think	I had to think hard to answer the math problem.
13.	ethnic	There are many different ethnic groups in my school.
14.	thicken	To thicken the batter, I added more flour.
15.	kitchen	

Sorts:

words containing "ch" sounds; words containing "th" sounds; words containing a silent letter; words that are nouns; words that are verbs

Transfer Words

	Words	Clue
1.	century	A century is a period of one hundred years.
2.	thankful	I am always thankful for my friends and family.
3.	knitting	My mom is knitting me a pair of socks.

Name _____

Making and Writing Words Worksheet

vowels	consonants

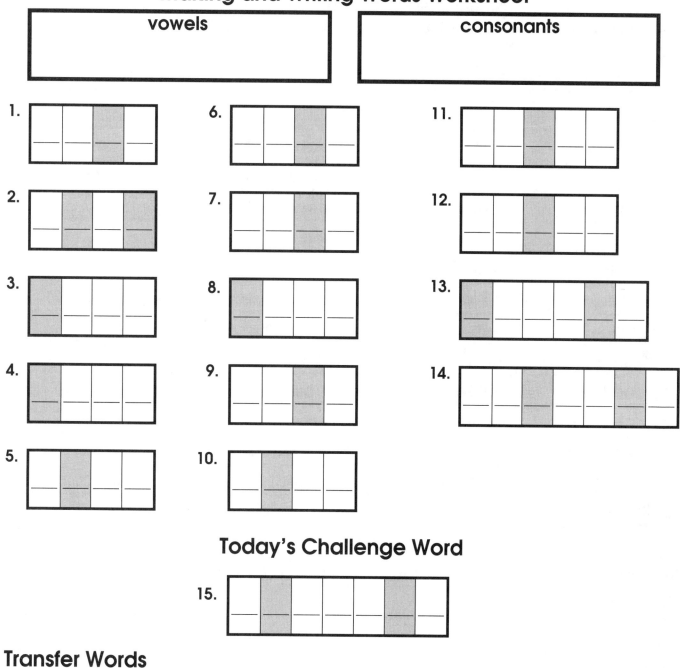

1.
6.
11.

2.
7.
12.

3.
8.
13.

4.
9.
14.

5.
10.

Today's Challenge Word

15.

Transfer Words

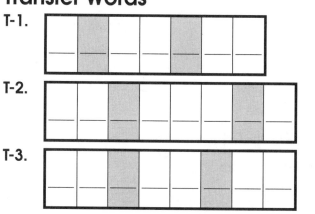

T-1.

T-2.

T-3.

Making and Writing Words Lesson
Challenge Word: machine

vowels a, e, i	consonants c, h, m, n

Making Words

Words	Sentence Clue
1. nice	The girl who shared her lunch with me is very nice.
2. each	I ride the bus to school each day.
3. inch	The screw for the desk is one inch long.
4. chin	My chin is at the bottom of my face.
5. cane	In the story we read, the old man walks with a cane.
6. came	Beth came to my birthday party late.
7. amen	At the end of a prayer, we often say "amen."
8. ache	I have a bad ache in my back.
9. manic	My excitable friend has a manic personality.
10. China	Our new neighbors are from China.
11. chime	We have a wind chime that makes a beautiful sound.
12. chain	The chain on my necklace broke.
13. iceman	Before refrigerators, the iceman delivered ice to homes.
14. cinema	I love to watch movies at our local cinema.
15. machine	

Sorts:
words containing "k" sounds; words containing long "a" sounds; words containing long "i" sounds; words containing a silent "e"

Transfer Words

Words	Clue
1. maniac	Sometimes, when I get excited, I feel like a maniac.
2. come	Will you please come to the store with me?
3. inchworm	I found an inchworm crawling up a tree in the yard.

Name _____

Making and Writing Words Worksheet

vowels	consonants

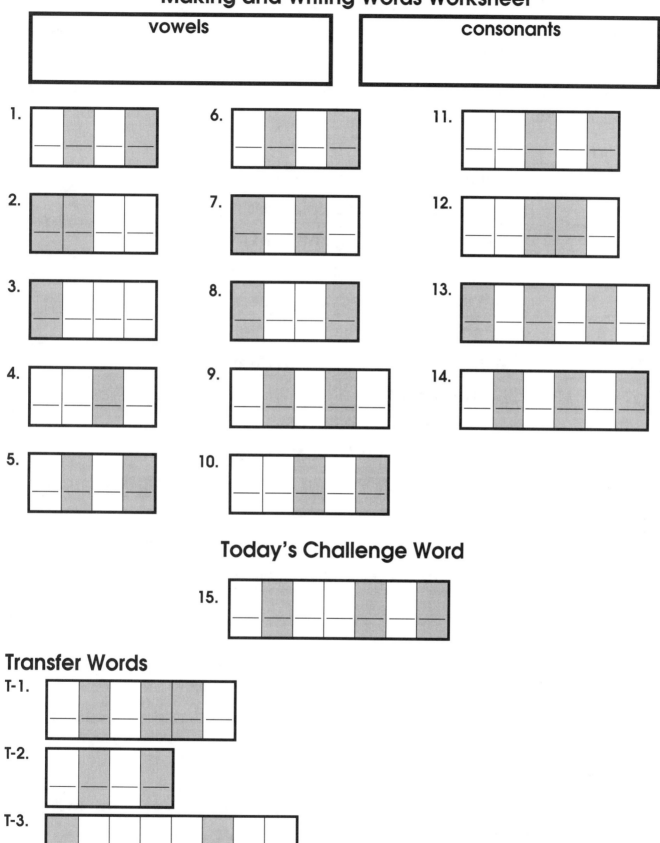

Today's Challenge Word

Transfer Words

31

Making and Writing Words Lesson
Challenge Word: private

vowels a, e, i	consonants p, r, t, v

Making Words

Words	Sentence Clue
1. art	During art class, I drew a picture of a flower.
2. part	Part of the board game is missing.
3. rip	When I was playing, I noticed a rip in my shirt.
4. trip	We went on a trip from Ohio to Georgia.
5. pave	The city plans to pave our street this summer.
6. rave	Disco music was the rave of the 70's.
7. ripe	A brown banana is too ripe to eat.
8. pair	My favorite pair of shoes are dark brown loafers.
9. tire	Our new car had a flat tire.
10. rate	The interest rate at the bank went up last week.
11. viper	I was almost bitten by a poisonous viper in the jungle.
12. rivet	The two pieces of steel were held together by a rivet.
13. avert	I often avert my eyes during scary movies.
14. pirate	The pirate had a peg leg and a patch over his eye.
15. private	

Sorts:
words that have words within them; words containing long "i" sounds; words containing a silent "e"; words that can be nouns or verbs

Transfer Words

Words	Clue
1. start	Before I could start the race, I had to stretch my legs.
2. tired	After I ran the race, I was very tired.
3. partner	Laura was my partner for the science project.

Name _____

Making and Writing Words Worksheet

vowels	consonants

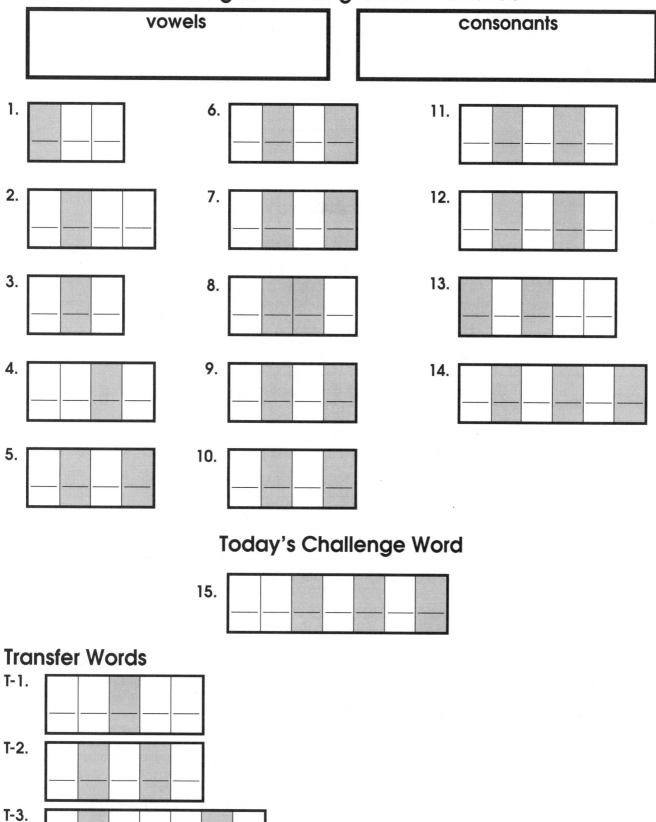

1.

6.

11.

2.

7.

12.

3.

8.

13.

4.

9.

14.

5.

10.

Today's Challenge Word

15.

Transfer Words

T-1.

T-2.

T-3.

Making and Writing Words Lesson
Challenge Word: alphabet

vowels	consonants
a, a, e	**b, h, l, p, t**

Making Words

	Words	Sentence Clue
1.	heal	I hope the scratch on my arm will heal quickly.
2.	pale	The sick child looked pale and tired.
3.	heap	The heap of clothes in my room has grown quite large.
4.	help	Can you help me with this homework problem?
5.	bath	Susan likes to take a bath in warm water.
6.	beat	To make the cake, Mom will beat the eggs with a spoon.
7.	belt	My dad wears a brown leather belt every day.
8.	tale	The tale about the princess and the knight was exciting.
9.	tape	I used clear tape to seal the storage boxes.
10.	table	I have a clock and a lamp on my bedroom table.
11.	plate	The dinner plate shattered when Bobby dropped it.
12.	petal	The rose petal was pink and smelled sweetly.
13.	leapt	The bullfrog leapt three feet across the floor.
14.	bathe	I bathe my dog at least once each month.
15.	alphabet	

Sorts:
words containing long "e" sounds; words containing long "a" sounds; words that are verbs; words that have homophones

Transfer Words

	Words	Clue
1.	bathroom	The bathroom in my house is on the first floor.
2.	pedal	When I ride my bike uphill, I have to pedal hard and fast.
3.	platter	At the party, food was served on a large silver platter.

34

Name _____

Making and Writing Words Worksheet

vowels	consonants

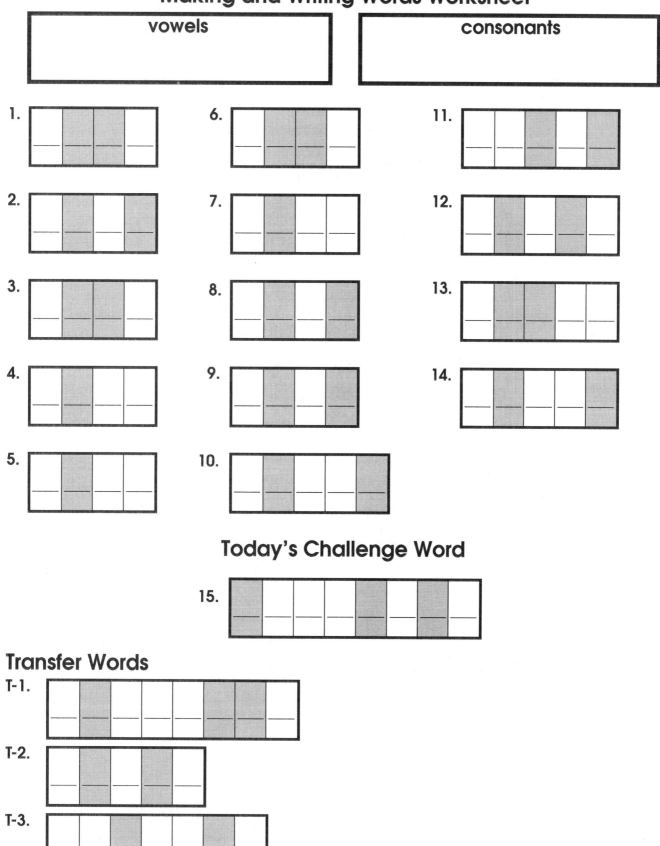

1.

6.

11.

2.

7.

12.

3.

8.

13.

4.

9.

14.

5.

10.

Today's Challenge Word

15.

Transfer Words

T-1.

T-2.

T-3.

Making and Writing Words Lesson
Challenge Word: aluminum

vowels	consonants
a, i, u, u	**l, m, m, n**

Making Words

	Words	Sentence Clue
1.	Al	My friend Al lives next door to me.
2.	an	An egg is an example of an oval.
3.	am	I am looking forward to summer vacation already.
4.	mum	The speechless mime was mum when asked questions.
5.	man	My brother was the best man in his friend's wedding.
6.	aim	Billy's aim with the water gun is not very accurate.
7.	Lima	The capital and largest city in Peru is called Lima.
8.	nail	I hammered the nail into the board.
9.	maul	Sometimes bears have been known to maul hikers.
10.	maim	It is illegal to hurt or maim animals.
11.	main	We had to identify the main idea of the paragraph.
12.	mail	We got only junk mail in our mailbox today.
13.	luau	Our class had a big luau to help us learn about Hawaii.
14.	alumni	Dan called the alumni together for a class reunion.
15.	aluminum	

Sorts:

1, 2, and 3+ syllable words; words containing short "a" sounds; words containing long "a" sounds

Transfer Words

	Words	Clue
1.	remain	The class had to remain silent during the fire drill.
2.	mummy	The mummy was buried in an ancient Egyptian tomb.
3.	maintain	The plane had to maintain a certain speed to take off.

Name _____

Making and Writing Words Worksheet

vowels	consonants

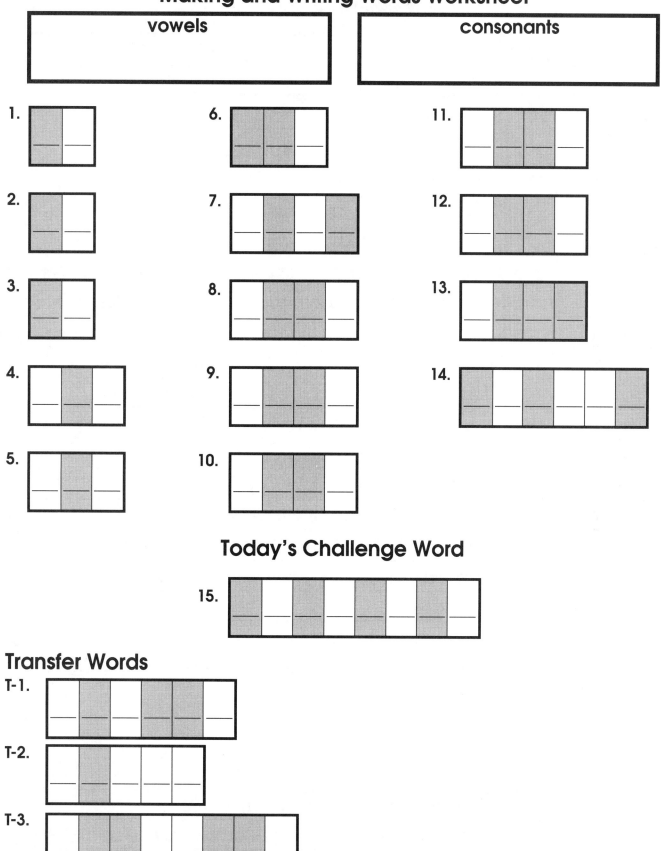

1.

2.

3.

4.

5.

6.

7.

8.

9.

10.

11.

12.

13.

14.

Today's Challenge Word

15.

Transfer Words

T-1.

T-2.

T-3.

Making and Writing Words Lesson
Challenge Word: astonish

vowels a, i, o	consonants h, n, s, s, t

Making Words

	Words	Sentence Clue
1.	this	This book belongs to my pal Sarah.
2.	thin	Plenty of exercise will keep you thin and in good shape.
3.	stash	I have a lot of candy hidden in my secret stash.
4.	shots	Dr. Morgan said that the shots would help me feel better.
5.	stain	My dad will stain the kitchen cabinets to match the floor.
6.	saint	She is so generous and good, she ought to be a saint.
7.	oaths	Everyone who wants to join the club must take two oaths.
8.	oasis	A fertile grassland in a desert is called an oasis.
9.	hosts	John and Joe were the hosts of the birthday party.
10.	hoist	The hoist broke and the bale of hay fell to the ground.
11.	hints	I gave my parents hints about birthday presents.
12.	satin	The satin dress was beautiful and elegant.
13.	stains	The muddy footprints left brown stains on the carpet.
14.	saints	Saints were very good and holy people.
15.	astonish	

Sorts:

1, 2, and 3 syllable words; words containing short "a" sounds; words that have words within them

Transfer Words

	Words	Clue
1.	think	I think that I did my best at school today.
2.	saintly	The girl who helped her grandpa acted in a saintly way.
3.	painter	The painter painted Dexter's room blue.

Name _____

Making and Writing Words Worksheet

vowels	consonants

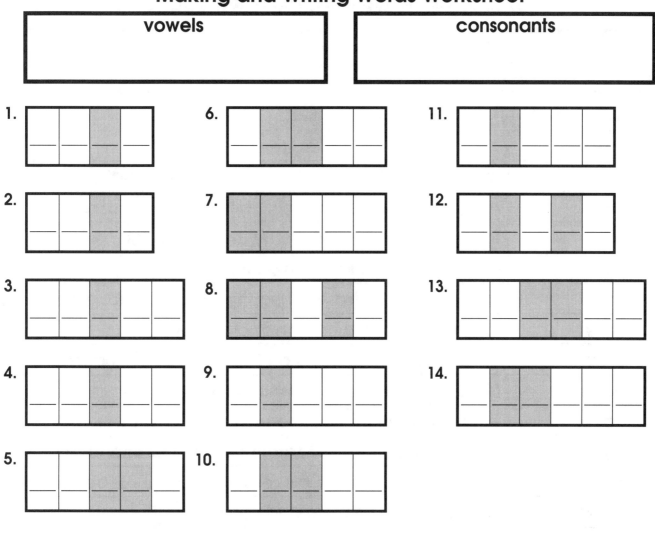

1.
2.
3.
4.
5.
6.
7.
8.
9.
10.
11.
12.
13.
14.

Today's Challenge Word

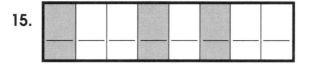

15.

Transfer Words

T-1.

T-2.

T-3.

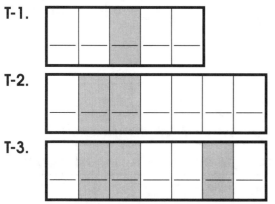

Making and Writing Words Lesson
Challenge Word: barnyard

vowels a, a	consonants b, d, n, r, r, y*

Making Words

	Words	Sentence Clue
1.	bay	The bay was filled with large, colorful sailboats.
2.	ray	A ray of sunlight came shining through the curtains.
3.	yard	The yard was too wet to play in after the rain.
4.	yarn	I learned how to knit with yarn.
5.	drab	The rainbow contrasted brightly with the drab, gray sky.
6.	darn	My mother likes to darn the holes in my socks.
7.	bran	My parents like to eat bran flakes cereal for breakfast.
8.	Brad	My favorite cousin is named Brad.
9.	barn	The horses live in a barn on my uncle's farm.
10.	band	There may be many different instruments in a band.
11.	radar	Radar helps track the movement of storms in our area.
12.	brand	What brand of soft drink do you like best?
13.	array	The array of different jets at the air show was impressive.
14.	Brandy	My friend's little sister is named Brandy.
15.	barnyard	

Sorts:

words containing consonant blends; words containing vowel digraphs; words containing long "a" sounds; words containing short "a" sounds; words that have other words within them

Transfer Words

	Words	Clue
1.	yardstick	A yardstick is a long ruler that measures up to three feet.
2.	stand	We had to stand when the judge entered the courtroom.
3.	standard	The dollar is the standard unit of money in the U.S.

Name _____

Making and Writing Words Worksheet

vowels	consonants

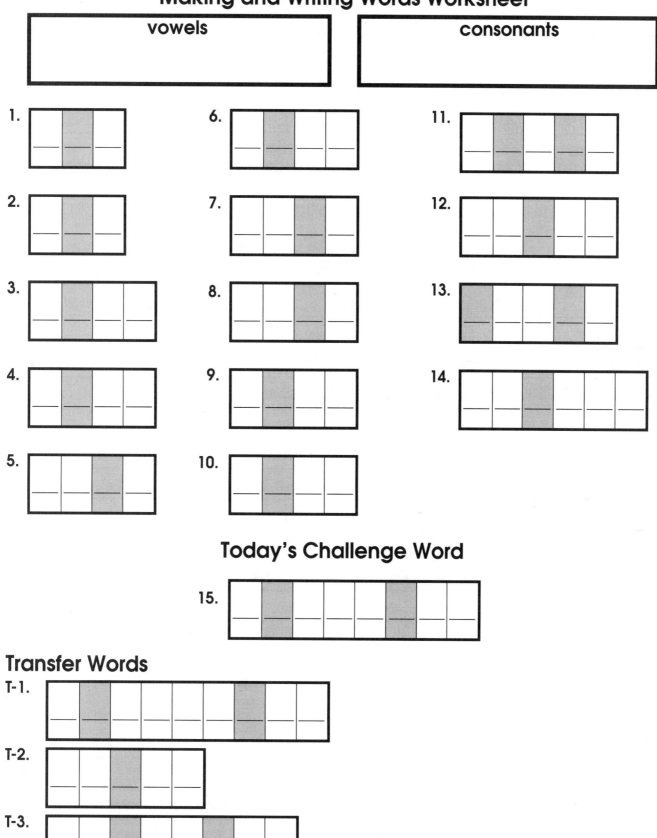

1.

2.

3.

4.

5.

6.

7.

8.

9.

10.

11.

12.

13.

14.

Today's Challenge Word

15.

Transfer Words

T-1.

T-2.

T-3.

41

Making and Writing Words Lesson
Challenge Word: carnival

vowels
a, a, i

consonants
c, l, n, r, v

Making Words

Words	Sentence Clue
1. rain	I love to walk in the rain.
2. vial	The vial contained an important medicine.
3. liar	A person who doesn't tell the truth is a liar.
4. Lara	My sister Lara is only three years old.
5. lava	Hot lava came spewing out of the erupting volcano.
6. clan	My dad calls our family his clan.
7. viral	My illness was caused by a viral infection.
8. rival	The rival team has several star players.
9. naval	That naval base is home to many large warships.
10. larva	The young fly was still in the form of a larva.
11. canal	The farmers dug a canal to bring water to their fields.
12. anvil	A blacksmith uses a hammer and anvil to shape metal.
13. racial	The town came together to support racial understanding.
14. caviar	Some people love to eat special fish eggs called caviar.
15. carnival	

Sorts:
1, 2, and 3 syllable words; words containing long "a" sounds; words containing long "i" sounds; words containing "al" sounds

Transfer Words

Words	Clue
1. clam	I found a clam while wading in the ocean.
2. dial	Older phones use a rotary dial instead of push buttons.
3. rivalry	The rivalry between the two football teams was intense.

Name _____

Making and Writing Words Worksheet

vowels	consonants

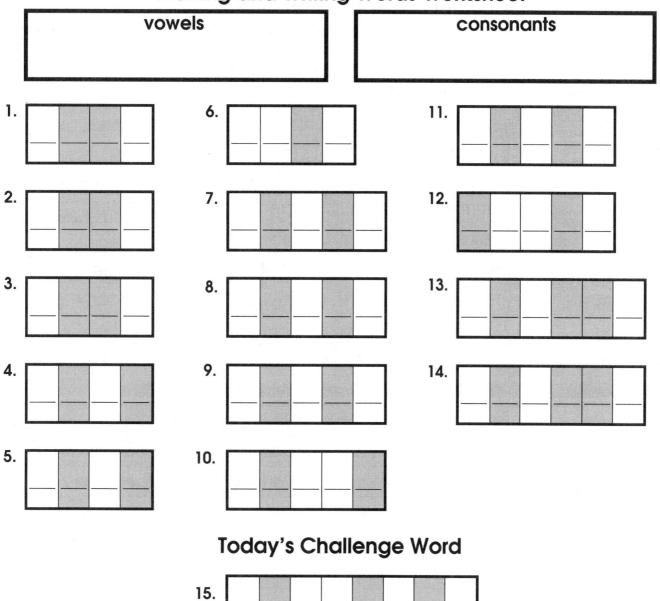

1.

2.

3.

4.

5.

6.

7.

8.

9.

10.

11.

12.

13.

14.

Today's Challenge Word

15.

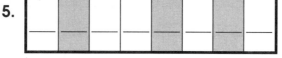

Transfer Words

T-1.

T-2.

T-3.

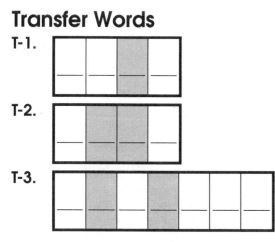

43

Making and Writing Words Lesson
Challenge Word: champion

vowels	consonants
a, i, o	**c, h, m, n, p**

Making Words

	Words	Sentence Clue
1.	coma	The man was in a coma for two weeks after his accident.
2.	coin	We settled the disagreement by flipping a coin.
3.	chip	The ceramic cup has a small chip in its side.
4.	camp	At camp, we set up our tents before we ate dinner.
5.	pinch	My brother got in trouble when he tried to pinch me.
6.	piano	I played a piano solo at our school's talent show.
7.	panic	We were proud that we did not panic during the fire drill.
8.	mocha	Mocha is a milkshake flavor that I really like.
9.	macho	The young boys tried to act like tough, macho men.
10.	china	We like to eat using the good china at Thanksgiving.
11.	chomp	The cows love to chomp on grass in the meadow.
12.	chimp	The chimp was kept in a cage until he was fully healed.
13.	champ	The champ was given an exceptionally large trophy.
14.	chain	Holding hands, we formed a chain around the room.
15.	champion	

Sorts:
1, 2, and 3 syllable words; words containing "ch" sounds; words containing long "o" sounds; words containing short "i" sounds

Transfer Words

	Words	Clue
1.	campsite	Our campsite was hidden away from the hiking trail.
2.	Chinese	We ate dinner at the new Chinese restaurant.
3.	chimpanzee	The chimpanzee lives in tropical parts of Africa.

Name _____

Making and Writing Words Worksheet

vowels	consonants

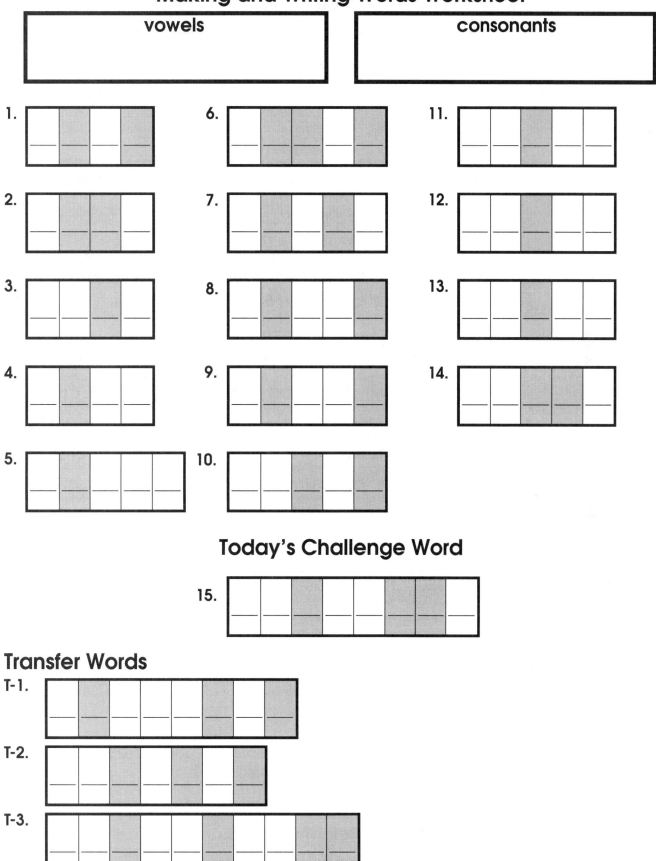

1.

2.

3.

4.

5.

6.

7.

8.

9.

10.

11.

12.

13.

14.

Today's Challenge Word

15.

Transfer Words

T-1.

T-2.

T-3.

Making and Writing Words Lesson
Challenge Word: creature

vowels	consonants
a, e, e, u	**c, r, r, t**

Making Words

	Words	Sentence Clue
1.	trace	Hardly a trace of the building was left after the explosion.
2.	truce	The boys stopped fighting and declared a truce.
3.	react	Do you react with anger when you hear bad news?
4.	racer	The autograph of that champion racer is valuable now.
5.	eater	When it comes to dessert, Beth is a fast eater.
6.	cuter	I think this puppy is cuter than all of the rest.
7.	crate	My new bicycle came packed in a wooden crate.
8.	cater	A restaurant will cater food and drinks for the wedding.
9.	acute	An acute angle is an angle of less than ninety degrees.
10.	crater	The crater on the moon was caused by an asteroid.
11.	create	I love to create art by drawing, painting, and sculpting.
12.	career	My mother has a successful career in business.
13.	terrace	The terrace was covered with trees, grass, and rocks.
14.	retrace	I will retrace my steps in order to find my lost keys.
15.	creature	

Sorts:

1, 2, and 3+ syllable words; words containing "er" sounds; words containing "s" sounds; words that have words within them; words containing consonant blends

Transfer Words

	Words	Clue
1.	cutest	My kitten is the cutest of them all.
2.	terrarium	My terrarium contains insects, plants, and a small turtle.
3.	creation	The artist's creation was truly inspiring.

Name _____

Making and Writing Words Worksheet

vowels	consonants

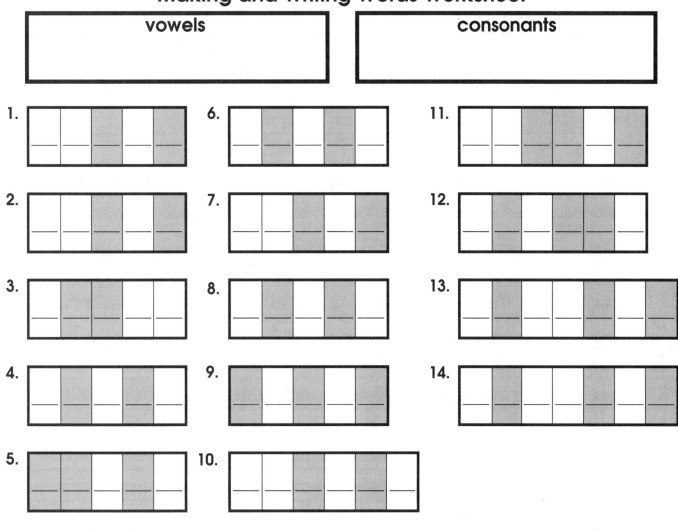

1.
2.
3.
4.
5.
6.
7.
8.
9.
10.
11.
12.
13.
14.

Today's Challenge Word

15.

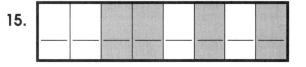

Transfer Words

T-1.

T-2.

T-3.

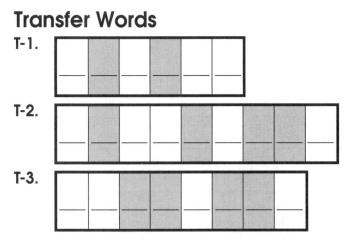

Making and Writing Words Lesson
Challenge Word: cupboard

vowels	consonants
a, o, u	**b, c, d, p, r**

Making Words

	Words	Sentence Clue
1.	drop	Tim plans to drop the water balloon out of the tall tree.
2.	prod	The farmer used a cattle prod to move the cows along.
3.	curb	Bonnie tripped and fell on the curb.
4.	crab	The crab scurried across the deserted beach.
5.	coup	The army started a coup to overthrow the government.
6.	cord	Jill plugged the television cord into the electrical outlet.
7.	carp	Dad took us fishing for carp at the pond.
8.	card	I bought a "get well soon" card for my sick friend.
9.	burp	I will help burp the baby after it has eaten.
10.	boar	A male pig is called a boar.
11.	proud	I am very proud of my dog for winning the contest.
12.	cobra	The cobra is a dangerous, poisonous snake.
13.	broad	Although the river is broad, it is only a few feet deep.
14.	board	After measuring it, Tom cut the board in half.
15.	cupboard	

Sorts:
1 and 2 syllable words; words containing consonant blends; words that can be both nouns and verbs

Transfer Words

	Words	Clue
1.	cordless	The cordless phone enables me to walk around and talk.
2.	proudest	My parents were proudest the day of the performance.
3.	crabby	If I stay up too late, I am often crabby the next day.

Name _____

Making and Writing Words Worksheet

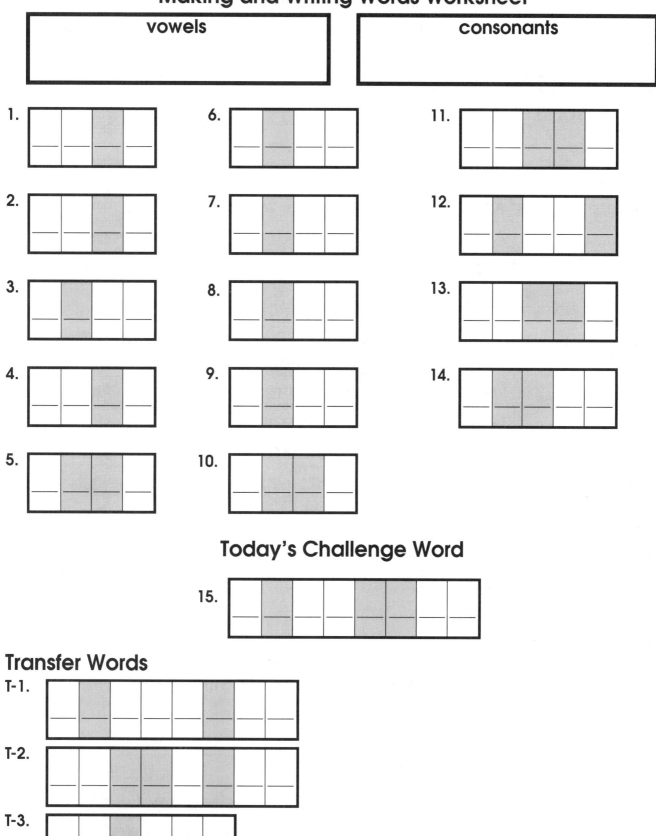

vowels	consonants

1.
2.
3.
4.
5.
6.
7.
8.
9.
10.
11.
12.
13.
14.

Today's Challenge Word

15.

Transfer Words

T-1.

T-2.

T-3.

Making and Writing Words Lesson
Challenge Word: daydream

vowels	consonants
a, a, e	**d, d, m, r, y***

Making Words

	Words	Sentence Clue
1.	year	Every year contains three hundred and sixty-five days.
2.	mare	A mare is a female horse, zebra, or donkey.
3.	dead	After the storm, I found a dead bird on the ground.
4.	dare	I would not dare to disobey my parents' instructions.
5.	dame	A dame is another name for a lady.
6.	army	The army is made up of many individual soldiers.
7.	ready	I am ready for a long vacation.
8.	dream	I sometimes dream of flying through the nighttime sky.
9.	dread	I really dread tomorrow's math test.
10.	drama	Is that new movie a comedy or a drama?
11.	dared	Kristen dared me to jump into the cold swimming pool.
12.	armed	The armed guards carried the money into the bank.
13.	dreamy	Erin thought that the boy from out of town was dreamy.
14.	madder	The wasps got madder as we approached their nest.
15.	daydream	

Sorts:

1, 2, and 3 syllable words; words containing short "e" sounds; words containing long "e" sounds; words that have words within them

Transfer Words

	Words	Clue
1.	dramatic	That movie star likes to play mostly dramatic roles.
2.	dreadful	We thought that the new movie was just dreadful.
3.	readiness	The team was in a state of readiness before the game.

Name _____

Making and Writing Words Worksheet

vowels	consonants

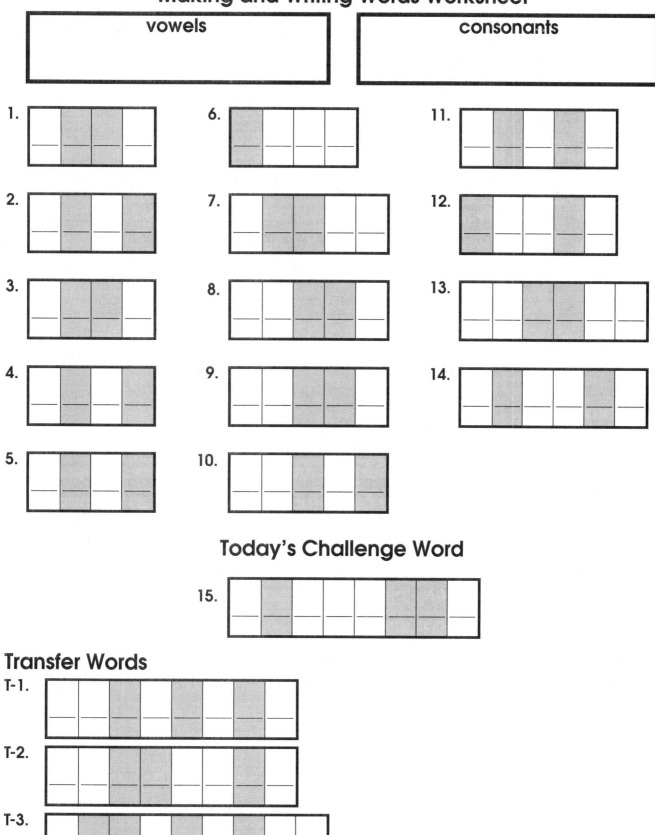

1.

6.

11.

2.

7.

12.

3.

8.

13.

4.

9.

14.

5.

10.

Today's Challenge Word

15.

Transfer Words

T-1.

T-2.

T-3.

Making and Writing Words Lesson
Challenge Word: elevator

vowels	consonants
a, e, e, o	**l, r, t, v**

Making Words

	Words	Sentence Clue
1.	valor	The soldier received a medal for his courage and valor.
2.	valet	Valet parking is available at the new restaurant.
3.	lever	I pulled the lever to make the race cars roll.
4.	leave	We will have to leave soon to get to the party on time.
5.	later	I plan to do my homework later in the afternoon.
6.	ravel	My sweater began to ravel during recess.
7.	avert	My dog will avert his eyes if he has done something bad.
8.	voter	Each voter casts his ballot in private.
9.	alter	Mom had to alter my sister's prom dress.
10.	alert	The siren will alert us if a tornado is on the way.
11.	travel	We plan to travel to California during spring break.
12.	revolt	The revolt against the government lasted only two days.
13.	reveal	We will reveal the winner's name at the art show tonight.
14.	relate	I can relate to the pain she feels from her uncle's death.
15.	elevator	

Sorts:
words containing "er" sounds; words containing long "a" sounds; words containing long "e" sounds; words containing a silent letter; words that have words within them

Transfer Words

	Words	Clue
1.	alteration	The seamstress made an alteration to the dress.
2.	relation	I have a distant relation who lives in Canada.
3.	revolution	The industrial revolution made America more productive.

Name _____

Making and Writing Words Worksheet

vowels	consonants

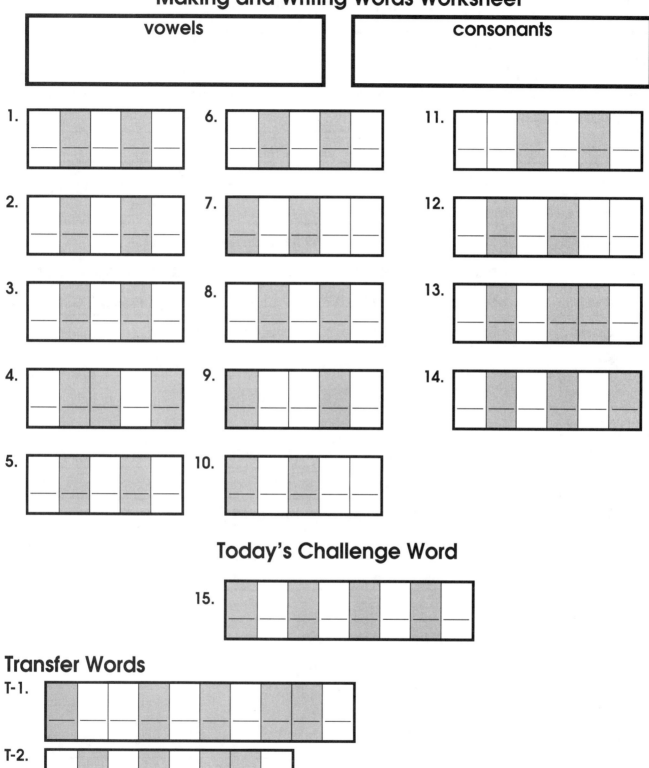

1.

2.

3.

4.

5.

6.

7.

8.

9.

10.

11.

12.

13.

14.

Today's Challenge Word

15.

Transfer Words

T-1.

T-2.

T-3.

Making and Writing Words Lesson
Challenge Word: enormous

vowels	consonants
e, o, o, u	**m, n, r, s**

Making Words

	Words	Sentence Clue
1.	sure	Are you sure that this is the dessert you want?
2.	snore	At night, I can hear my dad snore loudly.
3.	rooms	There are many rooms in that fancy hotel.
4.	nurse	My mother was a nurse before she was a schoolteacher.
5.	omens	Horseshoes and four-leaf clovers are good luck omens.
6.	norms	Our test scores were all above the school district norms.
7.	noose	The noose was made out of a thick rope.
8.	moose	The moose had very big antlers.
9.	moons	Some planets, such as Jupiter, have many moons.
10.	menus	The waiter gave us our menus after we were seated.
11.	sooner	Sooner or later, I will be able to get a pet.
12.	sermon	The preacher gave an inspired sermon on Sunday.
13.	mouser	That black cat is an excellent mouser.
14.	mourns	My sister's class mourns the loss of its pet hamster.
15.	enormous	

Sorts:
1, 2, and 3 syllable words; words containing "oo" sounds; words containing silent letters; words that have words within them

Transfer Words

	Words	Clue
1.	mournful	The mournful look on Karen's face told me she was sad.
2.	nursery	A garden nursery sells different kinds of plants and trees.
3.	normalcy	I look forward to a state of normalcy after school starts.

Name _____

Making and Writing Words Worksheet

vowels	consonants

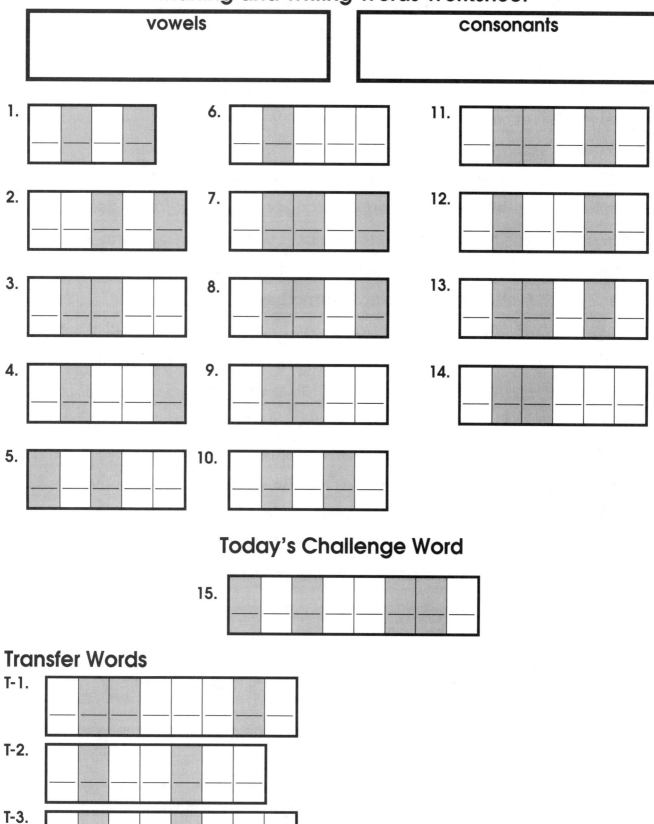

1.

6.

11.

2.

7.

12.

3.

8.

13.

4.

9.

14.

5.

10.

Today's Challenge Word

15.

Transfer Words

T-1.

T-2.

T-3.

Making and Writing Words Lesson
Challenge Word: festival

vowels **a, e, i**	consonants **f, l, s, t, v**

Making Words

	Words	Sentence Clue
1.	vial	The glass vial contains a top secret liquid.
2.	veal	My mother fixed veal chops for dinner last night.
3.	slave	The slave went to Canada on the Underground Railroad.
4.	stale	The stale bread was too hard and dry to eat.
5.	steal	It is wrong to steal from others.
6.	least	My easygoing dog is the least likely to bark at strangers.
7.	feast	Jenny's family enjoyed a huge Thanksgiving feast.
8.	alive	Alicia is so glad to be alive after falling off the roof.
9.	vital	The secret plans are of vital importance to the army.
10.	vilest	I think murderers are the vilest of criminals.
11.	valets	The valets parked all of the cars for the party guests.
12.	stifle	I tried to stifle a sneeze during the performance.
13.	itself	A wild animal knows how to take care of itself.
14.	fiesta	A fiesta is another name for a festival or party.
15.	festival	

Sorts:
1, 2, and 3+ syllable words; words containing long "e" sounds; words containing long "i" sounds; words that have words within them

Transfer Words

	Words	Clue
1.	stifling	The heat was stifling outside on Tuesday.
2.	revitalize	The city plans to revitalize its downtown areas.
3.	vitamin	Every morning, I get my vitamin C from orange juice.

Name _____

Making and Writing Words Worksheet

vowels	consonants

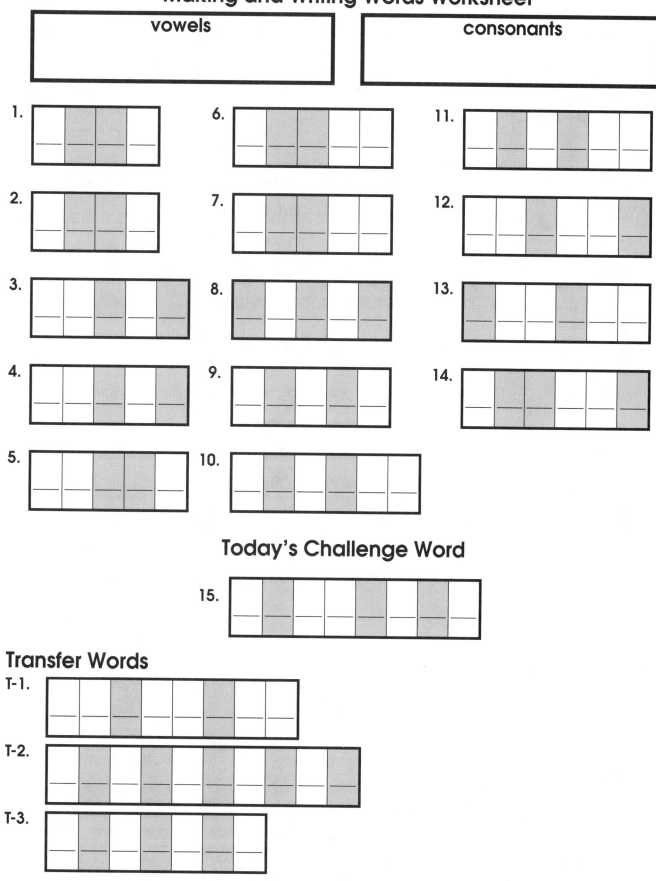

1.

2.

3.

4.

5.

6.

7.

8.

9.

10.

11.

12.

13.

14.

Today's Challenge Word

15.

Transfer Words

T-1.

T-2.

T-3.

Making and Writing Words Lesson
Challenge Word: guardian

vowels	consonants
a, a, i, u	**d, g, n, r**

Making Words

	Words	Sentence Clue
1.	ring	I helped my brother find a ring to give to his girlfriend.
2.	rain	My parents told me to come in out of the rain.
3.	rind	An orange rind is bitter to taste.
4.	rang	The telephone rang three times before I could answer it.
5.	Diana	My oldest cousin, Diana, was married last September.
6.	guard	The crossing guard at that intersection has to be alert.
7.	grind	It is not a good idea to grind your teeth.
8.	grand	The grand opening of the store is tomorrow morning.
9.	grain	The farmers store their grain in a silo.
10.	drain	It takes a long time to drain water from a swimming pool.
11.	again	I would love to ride that roller coaster again and again.
12.	iguana	An iguana is a type of lizard that may be kept as a pet.
13.	during	The lights went out during the severe thunderstorm.
14.	daring	The tightrope walker put on a very daring show.
15.	guardian	

Sorts:
words containing "ing" sounds; words containing long "a" sounds; words containing silent letters; words containing vowel digraphs

Transfer Words

	Words	Clue
1.	guarding	Many armed soldiers were guarding the entry to the fort.
2.	grinder	The butcher uses a meat grinder to make hamburger.
3.	drainage	The water drainage system keeps our yard from flooding.

Name _____

Making and Writing Words Worksheet

vowels	consonants

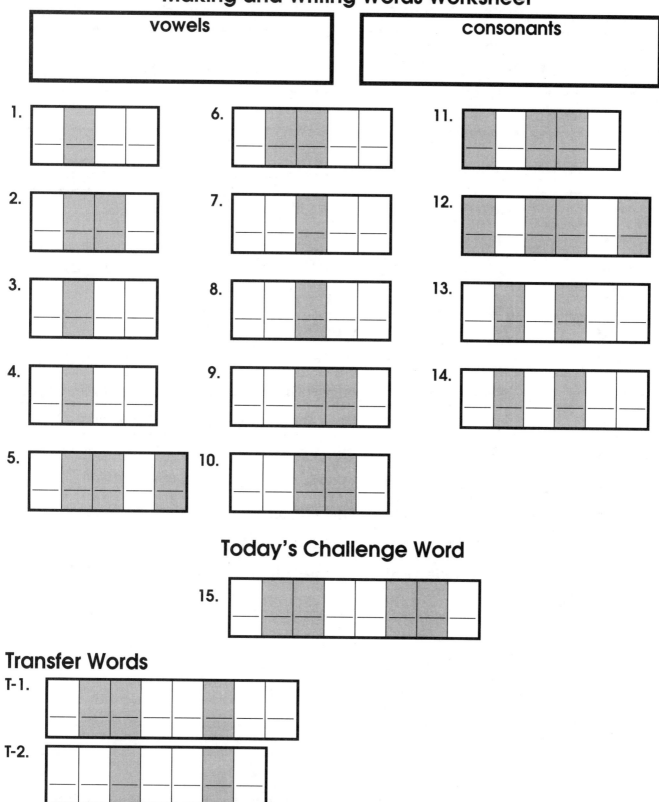

1.

2.

3.

4.

5.

6.

7.

8.

9.

10.

11.

12.

13.

14.

Today's Challenge Word

15.

Transfer Words

T-1.

T-2.

T-3.

Making and Writing Words Lesson
Challenge Word: magician

vowels	consonants
a, a, i, i	**c, g, m, n**

Making Words

	Words	Sentence Clue
1.	nag	My friend likes to nag everyone she meets.
2.	aim	Steve had to aim carefully to hit the bull's-eye.
3.	man	That man is a teacher at my school.
4.	can	Sally can make almost anything out of modeling clay.
5.	mica	Mica is an unusual, shiny type of mineral.
6.	mini	Mini skirts are very popular this year.
7.	Main	In my hometown, Main Street has many large buildings.
8.	gain	My brother will gain weight if he keeps eating junk food.
9.	mania	The band created a music mania when it performed.
10.	magic	I find magic shows to be very entertaining.
11.	icing	The icing on the cake was pink and white.
12.	again	Susie cried when she fell on her knee again.
13.	maniac	He drove his car like a maniac.
14.	aiming	Sally was aiming for the target but missed.
15.	magician	

Sorts:
1, 2, and 3 syllable words; words containing long "a" sounds; words containing vowel digraphs; words that have words within them

Transfer Words

	Words	Clue
1.	magical	The fireworks display seemed almost magical to me.
2.	mainstay	Agriculture is a mainstay of the economy.
3.	canning	Last week, mother was canning tomatoes for winter.

Name _____

Making and Writing Words Worksheet

vowels	consonants

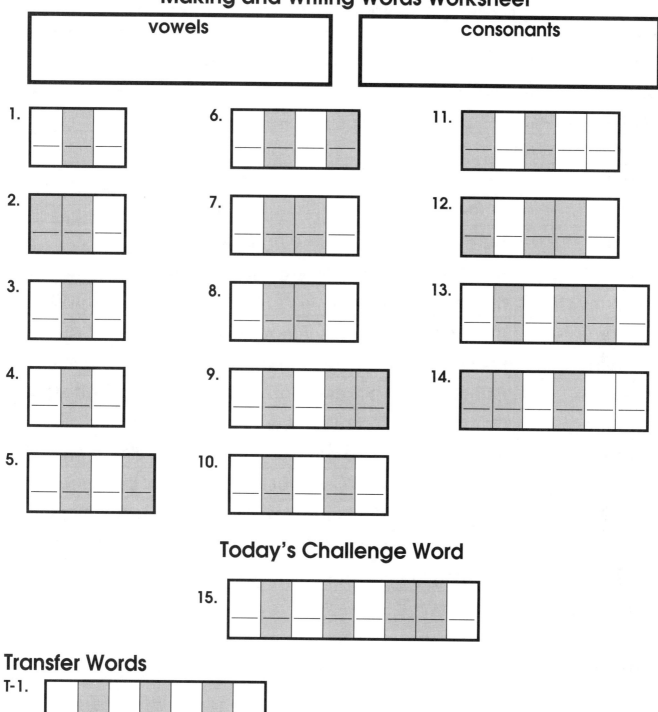

1.
2.
3.
4.
5.
6.
7.
8.
9.
10.
11.
12.
13.
14.

Today's Challenge Word

15.

Transfer Words

T-1.

T-2.

T-3.

Making and Writing Words Lesson
Challenge Word: marathon

vowels a, a, o	consonants h, m, n, r, t

Making Words

	Words	Sentence Clue
1.	oath	My best friend and I swore an oath never to fight again.
2.	moat	The water-filled moat protected the castle from invaders.
3.	moan	The injured animal would moan every few minutes.
4.	horn	The rhino at the zoo has a big, sharp horn.
5.	harm	My mother told me never to harm people or animals.
6.	atom	The atom bomb was very powerful and destructive.
7.	thorn	I pricked my finger on a thorn while I was cutting roses.
8.	north	Canada is the country located north of the United States.
9.	month	Courtney's birthday is in the month of October.
10.	manor	In olden days, a large house was often called a manor.
11.	aroma	The aroma of the flowers attracted a lot of bumblebees.
12.	aorta	The aorta is an artery that supplies blood to the body.
13.	matron	His wife had reached the age to be called a matron.
14.	Martha	Martha Washington's birthday is in June.
15.	marathon	

Sorts:

words containing "or" sounds; words containing long "o" sounds; words containing consonant digraphs; words that have words within them

Transfer Words

	Words	Clue
1.	charm	The likable boy has a lot of charm and good manners.
2.	harmless	The cute little puppy is harmless.
3.	matronly	The well-dressed older woman seemed rather matronly.

Name _____

Making and Writing Words Worksheet

vowels	consonants

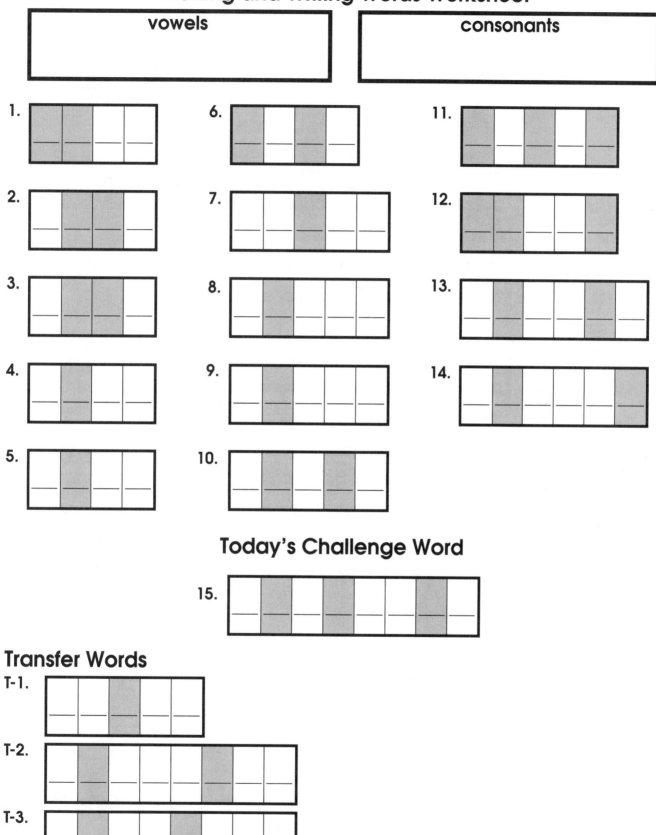

1.

6.

11.

2.

7.

12.

3.

8.

13.

4.

9.

14.

5.

10.

Today's Challenge Word

15.

Transfer Words

T-1.

T-2.

T-3.

Making and Writing Words Lesson

Challenge Word: nuisance

vowels	consonants
a, e, i, u	**c, n, n, s**

Making Words

	Words	Sentence Clue
1.	cue	The director will cue you when it is time to begin.
2.	scan	Dad likes to scan TV channels with the remote control.
3.	nine	There are nine players on a baseball team.
4.	nice	The man was nice and kind to everyone he met.
5.	case	We drank a whole case of soda at the party.
6.	cane	I found a candy cane in my Christmas stocking.
7.	acne	It is common for teenagers to get acne on their faces.
8.	aces	There are four aces in a deck of cards.
9.	since	The grass has been soggy since the rainstorm last night.
10.	sauce	We made a tasty sauce using tomatoes from our garden.
11.	canes	My grandma and grandpa both use canes to walk.
12.	cause	The cause of the accident is still under investigation.
13.	insane	The crowd went insane when the teams ran on the field.
14.	canine	A canine is another word for a dog.
15.	nuisance	

Sorts:

1, 2, and 3+ syllable words; words containing "s" sounds; words that are nouns; words containing a silent "e"

Transfer Words

	Words	Clue
1.	because	I had to go to the store because we were out of milk.
2.	insanity	The men said the plan to rob the bank was pure insanity.
3.	scanner	We hooked up a scanner to our computer today.

Name _____

Making and Writing Words Worksheet

vowels	consonants

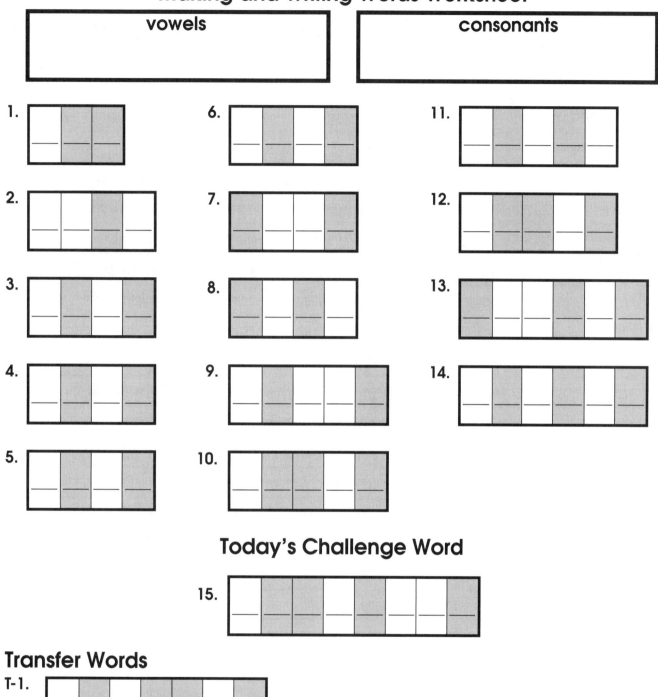

1.
2.
3.
4.
5.
6.
7.
8.
9.
10.
11.
12.
13.
14.

Today's Challenge Word

15.

Transfer Words

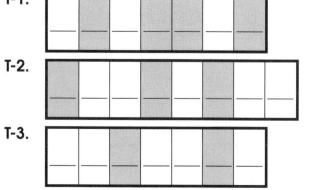

T-1.
T-2.
T-3.

Making and Writing Words Lesson
Challenge Word: ordinary

vowels a, i, o	consonants d, n, r, r, y*

Making Words

	Words	Sentence Clue
1.	roar	Lions roar when they are protecting their territory.
2.	road	The black asphalt road gets hot during the summer.
3.	rain	Our baseball game was cancelled due to rain.
4.	raid	In the summer, ants love to raid picnic baskets.
5.	iron	Mom will iron my clothes if they are wrinkled.
6.	arid	The desert was dry, dusty, and arid.
7.	rainy	The rainy day was cold and dark.
8.	rayon	Nylon and rayon are synthetic, or man-made, fibers.
9.	radio	I turned on my radio to listen to the news.
10.	drain	The water in the sink went down the drain quickly.
11.	diary	I write my secrets in my diary every day.
12.	dairy	I went to the dairy section of the store to buy some milk.
13.	adorn	We plan to adorn our Christmas tree with new ornaments.
14.	ordain	The bishop will ordain five new ministers this year.
15.	ordinary	

Sorts:
words containing long "e" sounds; words containing long "a" sounds; words containing "or" sounds

Transfer Words

	Words	Clue
1.	adore	I adore my new baby sister.
2.	drainage	The new drainage system prevents flooding in the town.
3.	crayon	I outlined my sketch with a black crayon.

Name _____

Making and Writing Words Worksheet

vowels	consonants

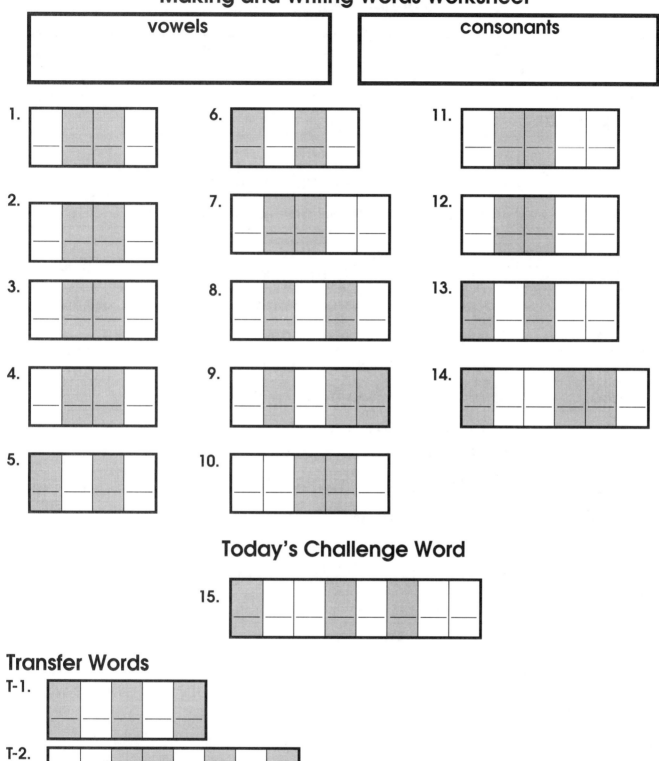

Today's Challenge Word

15.

Transfer Words

T-1.

T-2.

T-3.

Making and Writing Words Lesson
Challenge Word: pamphlet

vowels	consonants
a, e	**h, l, m, p, p, t**

Making Words

Words	Sentence Clue
1. lamp	My brother broke the lamp in the living room.
2. pale	The room was painted pale blue and green.
3. male	All men and boys are of the male gender.
4. helm	The captain stood at the helm of the ship.
5. help	If you have time, I need some help with this assignment.
6. leap	Jerry dared me to leap across the mud puddle.
7. late	Stephanie was late for the slumber party.
8. plate	Terry broke her mother's favorite plate.
9. petal	I watched as the rose petal fell lightly to the ground.
10. metal	Trash cans can be made of metal or plastic.
11. maple	Mrs. Ellis gave us a bottle of her homemade maple syrup.
12. leapt	Mary leapt over the creek without getting wet.
13. apple	I ate the red, juicy apple in less than two minutes.
14. ample	We have an ample supply of apples this year.
15. pamphlet	

Sorts:

1, 2, and 3 syllable words; words containing "ul" sounds; words containing short "a" sounds; words containing a silent "e"; words that have words within them; words that have homophones

Transfer Words

Words	Clue
1. platter	At the party, we served the vegetables on a platter.
2. metallic	My sister's new car is metallic blue in color.
3. trample	A herd of elephants could trample anything in its path.

Name _____

Making and Writing Words Worksheet

vowels	consonants

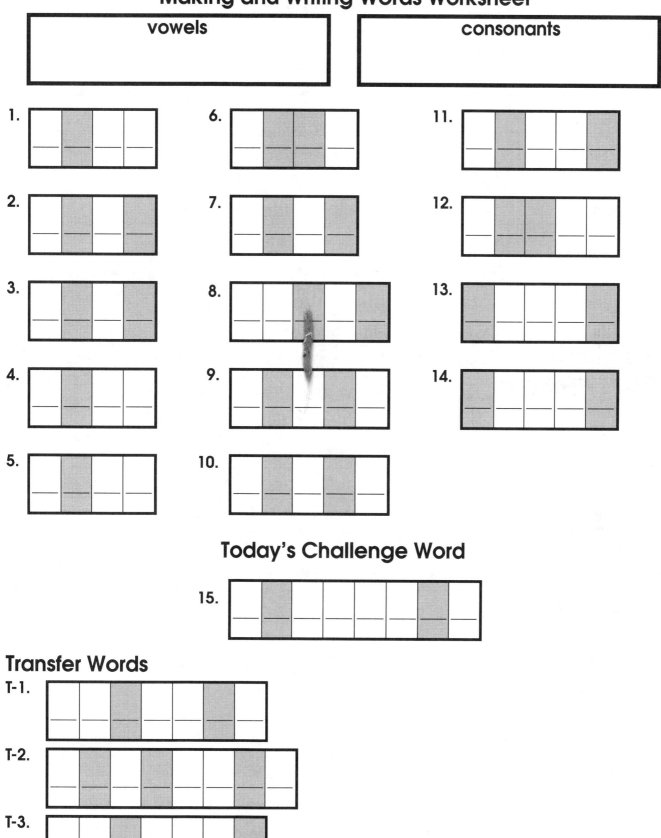

1.

6.

11.

2.

7.

12.

3.

8.

13.

4.

9.

14.

5.

10.

Today's Challenge Word

15.

Transfer Words

T-1.

T-2.

T-3.

69

Making and Writing Words Lesson
Challenge Word: parakeet

vowels a, a, e, e	consonants k, p, r, t

Making Words

	Words	Sentence Clue
1.	peek	Maria was tempted to peek at her birthday presents.
2.	keep	I keep my goldfish in a large glass bowl.
3.	rake	In the fall, I have to rake leaves often.
4.	rate	That ambulance is driving at a fast rate of speed.
5.	reek	Those dogs reek with the smell of skunk.
6.	tree	I think that the oak tree has the prettiest leaves.
7.	taper	We started with hard exercises, then began to taper off.
8.	taker	There was only one taker for our used car.
9.	parka	A parka is a heavy coat worn in cold weather.
10.	eaten	I have eaten all the popcorn in the bowl.
11.	apart	That old chair has fallen apart three times this week.
12.	retake	The teacher said that we could retake the math quiz.
13.	karate	My brother is taking karate lessons for self defense.
14.	partake	We partake of good food at every meal.
15.	parakeet	

Sorts:

1, 2, and 3 syllable words; words containing long "e" sounds; words containing a silent "e"; words that have words within them

Transfer Words

	Words	Clue
1.	apartment	My family lives in an apartment instead of a house.
2.	taking	I told Dad that I am taking the garbage out tonight.
3.	eating	We will be eating in less than one hour.

Name _____

Making and Writing Words Worksheet

vowels	consonants

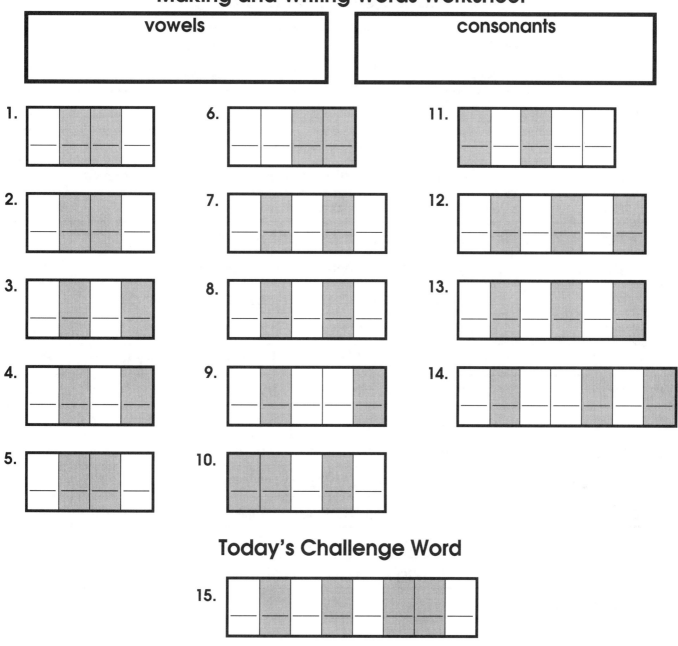

1.
2.
3.
4.
5.

6.
7.
8.
9.
10.

11.
12.
13.
14.

Today's Challenge Word

15.

Transfer Words

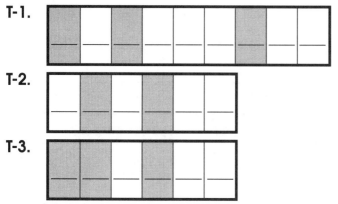

T-1.

T-2.

T-3.

Making and Writing Words Lesson
Challenge Word: pleasure

vowels	consonants
a, e, e, u	**l, p, r, s**

Making Words

	Words	Sentence Clue
1.	sure	Suzanne is sure that she will win the talent show.
2.	slur	When I speak too fast, I slur my words.
3.	slurp	I noisily slurp my soup from my spoon.
4.	sleep	The sound of rain falling helps me to sleep.
5.	leap	I can leap farther than anyone else in my class.
6.	real	That is a real antique, not a reproduction.
7.	reel	When I catch a fish, I reel it in with my new fishing rod.
8.	elapse	There are five minutes left to elapse on the timer.
9.	please	To be polite, say "please" when asking for something.
10.	pearls	Pearls are formed inside oysters.
11.	asleep	When I am tired, I fall asleep easily.
12.	repulse	The army hopes to repulse its enemy in the next battle.
13.	repeal	The citizens want to repeal the unfair law.
14.	relapse	I was feeling better, but I think I am having a relapse.
15.	pleasure	

Sorts:

words containing a silent "e"; words containing long "e" sounds; words containing "er" sounds; words that have words within them

Transfer Words

	Words	Clue
1.	surely	If you study hard, you will surely get a good grade.
2.	sleepy	I get very sleepy whenever I stay up too late.
3.	reality	Unicorns do not exist in reality.

Name _____

Making and Writing Words Worksheet

vowels	consonants

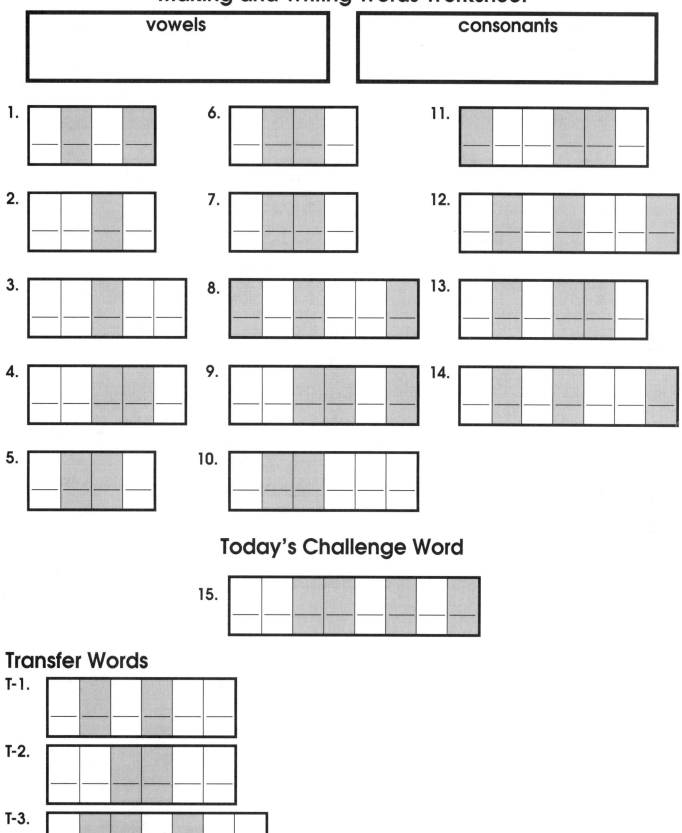

1.

2.

3.

4.

5.

6.

7.

8.

9.

10.

11.

12.

13.

14.

Today's Challenge Word

15.

Transfer Words

T-1.

T-2.

T-3.

Making and Writing Words Lesson
Challenge Word: reporter

vowels	consonants
e, e, o	**p, r, r, r, t**

Making Words

	Words	Sentence Clue
1.	toe	I stubbed my toe while running without shoes.
2.	tee	I hit the golf ball off the tee.
3.	pro	I hope to become a pro basketball player someday.
4.	tree	The tree in our backyard provides a lot of shade.
5.	tore	I tore my new pants on the playground today.
6.	rope	The rope connecting the swing to the tree branch broke.
7.	port	The huge ship slowly pulled into port.
8.	poet	Shel Silverstein is my favorite poet.
9.	peer	I watched the puppy peer around the corner at the cat.
10.	Peter	My next door neighbor's name is Peter.
11.	error	Heather made one error on her homework assignment.
12.	report	Tim's report on airplanes was the best in the class.
13.	terror	The horror movie was filled with screams of terror.
14.	porter	The porter carried our luggage from the car to the train.
15.	reporter	

Sorts:

1, 2, and 3 syllable words; words containing "or" sounds; words containing long "o" sounds; words containing a silent "e"; words referring to people

Transfer Words

	Words	Clue
1.	poetry	I enjoy writing and reading good poetry.
2.	airport	Fog closed the airport to all incoming flights.
3.	terrorize	We will terrorize the customers of our haunted house.

Name _____

Making and Writing Words Worksheet

vowels	consonants

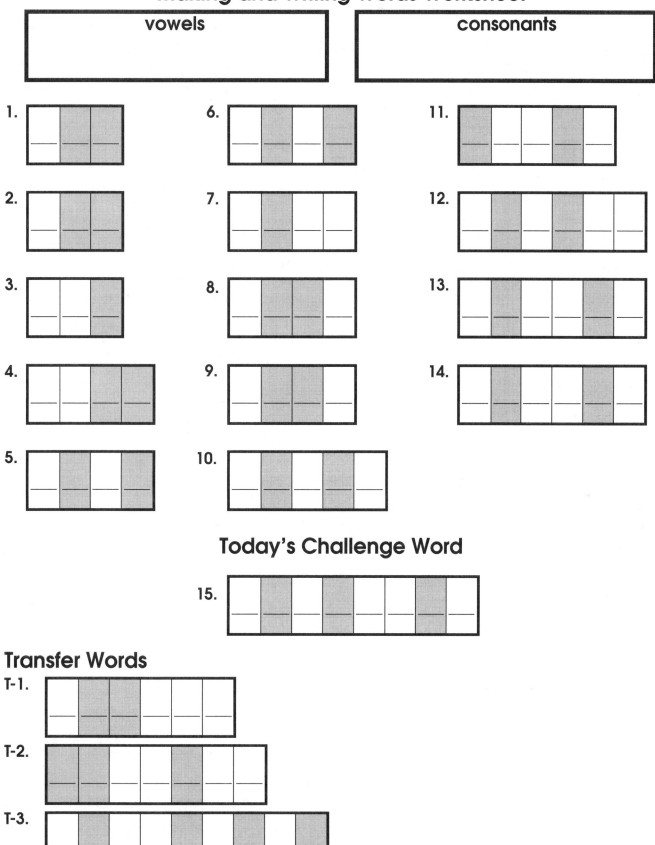

Today's Challenge Word

15.

Transfer Words

T-1.

T-2.

T-3.

Making and Writing Words Lesson
Challenge Word: sandwich

vowels **a, i**	consonants **c, d, h, n, s, w**

Making Words

Words	Sentence Clue
1. aid	Lisa needed first aid after she hurt her arm.
2. said	John said that he would bring cookies to the party.
3. sand	Sand at the beach can become very hot.
4. hand	I enjoy giving a helping hand to my friends.
5. wand	In the story, the fairy godmother waved her magic wand.
6. dash	When I am running late, I have to dash to the bus stop.
7. dish	My favorite Italian dish is spaghetti with meatballs.
8. winds	When the storms came up, the winds blew very hard.
9. wands	I pretended the sticks were wands with magical powers.
10. hands	Before I eat, I always wash my hands.
11. dawn	At dawn, we watched a beautiful sunrise.
12. chins	The children's chins were dirty after playing outside.
13. china	Our china dishes are used only on special occasions.
14. chains	Dad used chains to pull the old car to the repair shop.
15. sandwich	

Sorts:

words containing short "i" sounds; words that are plural; words containing consonant digraphs

Transfer Words

Words	Clue
1. pawn	The pawn is the most common piece in a chess set.
2. handsome	My brother looks very handsome when he dresses up.
3. dishpan	The dishpan was full of dirty dishes to be washed.

Name _____

Making and Writing Words Worksheet

vowels	consonants

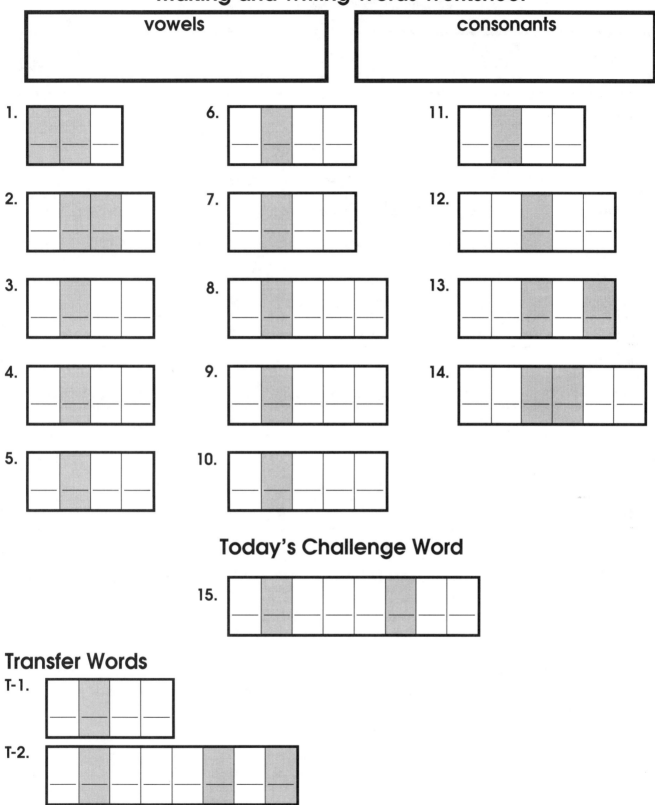

Today's Challenge Word

Transfer Words

Making and Writing Words Lesson
Challenge Word: sculpture

vowels	consonants
e, u, u	**c, l, p, r, s, t**

Making Words

	Words	Sentence Clue
1.	true	The movie was based on a true story.
2.	spurt	The sudden spurt of water from the hose surprised Todd.
3.	truce	The two armies ended their fighting with a solemn truce.
4.	ulcer	An ulcer is a sore in the stomach.
5.	cruel	The villain of the story was cruel and evil.
6.	spruce	We planted a spruce tree in our yard this weekend.
7.	rustle	I love to hear the leaves on the ground rustle as I walk.
8.	result	As a result of the rainstorm, the ground was all soggy.
9.	pursue	After high school, I will pursue a college degree.
10.	purest	The mountain lake had the purest water I have seen.
11.	luster	The newly minted coins had a bright luster.
12.	erupts	That volcano erupts every ten to twenty years.
13.	cluster	There was one ripe cluster of grapes left on the vine.
14.	culture	Baseball and hot dogs are part of the American culture.
15.	sculpture	

Sorts:

words containing "er" sounds; words containing long "u" sounds; words containing consonant blends; words containing suffixes or inflected endings; superlative adjectives (ending with "est")

Transfer Words

	Words	Clue
1.	truest	Emily, my truest friend, keeps all my secrets.
2.	eruption	The volcanic eruption was loud and fiery.
3.	pursuing	I am pursuing my dream to become a teacher.

Name _____

Making and Writing Words Worksheet

vowels	consonants

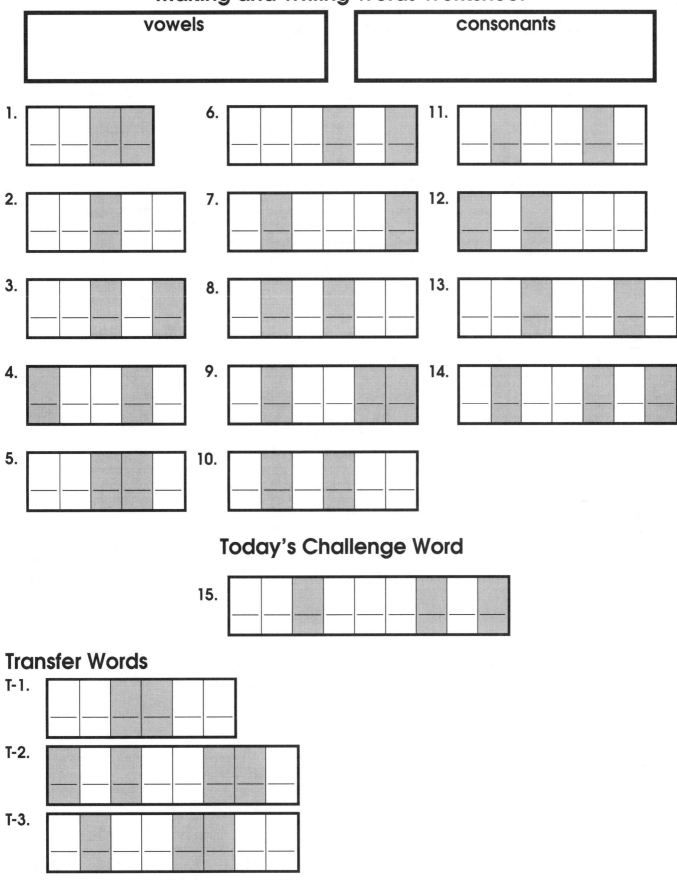

1.
2.
3.
4.
5.

6.
7.
8.
9.
10.

11.
12.
13.
14.

Today's Challenge Word

15.

Transfer Words

T-1.

T-2.

T-3.

Making and Writing Words Lesson
Challenge Word: skeleton

vowels	consonants
e, e, o	**k, l, n, s, t**

Making Words

	Words	Sentence Clue
1.	sent	My mom sent my older brother to the store.
2.	tense	Everyone felt quite tense after the argument.
3.	stole	I think my sister stole a look at my journal.
4.	sleet	Sleet is made up of tiny balls of ice and rain.
5.	sleek	The car looked sleek and shiny after we polished it.
6.	onset	The onset of winter is about a month after Thanksgiving.
7.	notes	In class, we took notes about mammals.
8.	knots	My sister tied her shoe strings into several knots.
9.	knelt	I knelt beside my desk to pick up my pencil.
10.	knees	I skinned my knees when I fell down.
11.	tokens	I paid for the bus trip with tokens.
12.	stolen	The stolen car was found the next day.
13.	nestle	The sleepy baby tried to nestle her head on my shoulder.
14.	kneels	In the story, the knight kneels before the king and queen.
15.	skeleton	

Sorts:
1 and 2 syllable words; words containing consonant blends; words containing long "e" sounds; words containing silent letters

Transfer Words

	Words	Clue
1.	nestling	My dog and I were nestling on the couch.
2.	tension	There was a lot of tension in the room before the test.
3.	wrestle	Children are not allowed to fight and wrestle at recess.

Name _____

Making and Writing Words Worksheet

vowels	consonants

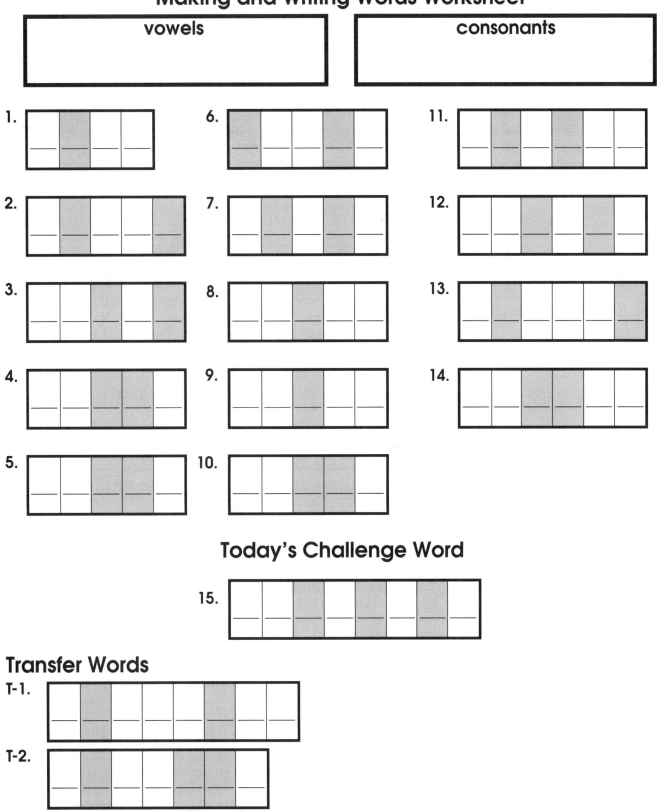

1.

2.

3.

4.

5.

6.

7.

8.

9.

10.

11.

12.

13.

14.

Today's Challenge Word

15.

Transfer Words

T-1.

T-2.

T-3.

81

Making and Writing Words Lesson
Challenge Word: stranger

vowels	consonants
a, e	**g, n, r, r, s, t**

Making Words

	Words	Sentence Clue
1.	stage	The stage was filled with singers and dancers.
2.	stare	He continued to stare at me throughout the class.
3.	anger	It was easy to see the anger on his face.
4.	great	My sister is always coming up with great ideas for gifts.
5.	gates	The front gates to the mansion open automatically.
6.	grate	The screen doors grate against the rusty hinges.
7.	grater	I used a grater to shred the cheese.
8.	grants	I wrote a story in which a genie grants me three wishes.
9.	arrest	I hope that the police arrest the escaped criminals soon.
10.	angers	It angers me when I know that people are not listening.
11.	agents	The agents visiting our mayor are from the FBI.
12.	strange	The new dog in the neighborhood has a strange bark.
13.	ranger	The forest ranger protects all the animals in the park.
14.	garnet	A garnet is a semiprecious stone that is red in color.
15.	stranger	

Sorts:

words containing "er" sounds; words containing long "a" sounds; words that have words within them; words that can be both nouns and verbs

Transfer Words

	Words	Clue
1.	strangest	Joey's ideas about aliens are the strangest I have heard.
2.	agency	The pet adoption agency helped us find a new puppy.
3.	greatness	The Olympic champion's greatness was undeniable.

Name _____

Making and Writing Words Worksheet

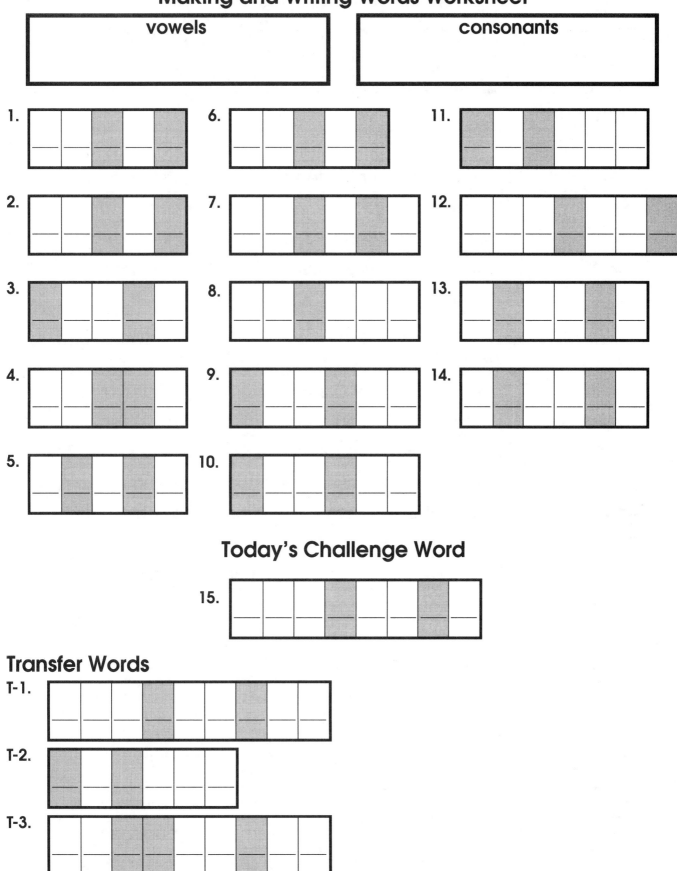

| vowels | consonants |

1.

2.

3.

4.

5.

6.

7.

8.

9.

10.

11.

12.

13.

14.

Today's Challenge Word

15.

Transfer Words

T-1.

T-2.

T-3.

83

Making and Writing Words Lesson
Challenge Word: sympathy

vowels	consonants
a	h, m, p, s, t, y*, y*

Making Words

	Words	Sentence Clue
1.	say	I thought it was nice to say "hello" to the new student.
2.	yam	A yam is a vegetable that is like a sweet potato.
3.	pays	It pays to study and do your homework every day.
4.	past	In the past, I used training wheels on my bicycle.
5.	taps	The band leader taps his foot with the music.
6.	spat	I got into a spat with my sister over what movie to see.
7.	path	Emily and Kerry like to hike on the path in the woods.
8.	math	In math class, we are learning how to multiply.
9.	myth	I read a myth about the Greek goddess Athena.
10.	stamp	I put a postage stamp on the letter before I mailed it.
11.	paths	We followed many different paths during our bike ride.
12.	pasty	When Bill was sick, his complexion was pale and pasty.
13.	myths	We read myths about many Greek gods and goddesses.
14.	hasty	We made a hasty retreat from the angry wasps.
15.	sympathy	

Sorts:

words containing "th" sounds; words containing long vowel sounds; words containing short "a" sounds; words containing consonant blends

Transfer Words

	Words	Clue
1.	pathway	The pathway to my house is bordered with flowers.
2.	stump	After chopping down the tree, we dug up the stump.
3.	splatter	I had to be careful not to splatter my shirt with sauce.

Name _____

Making and Writing Words Worksheet

vowels	consonants

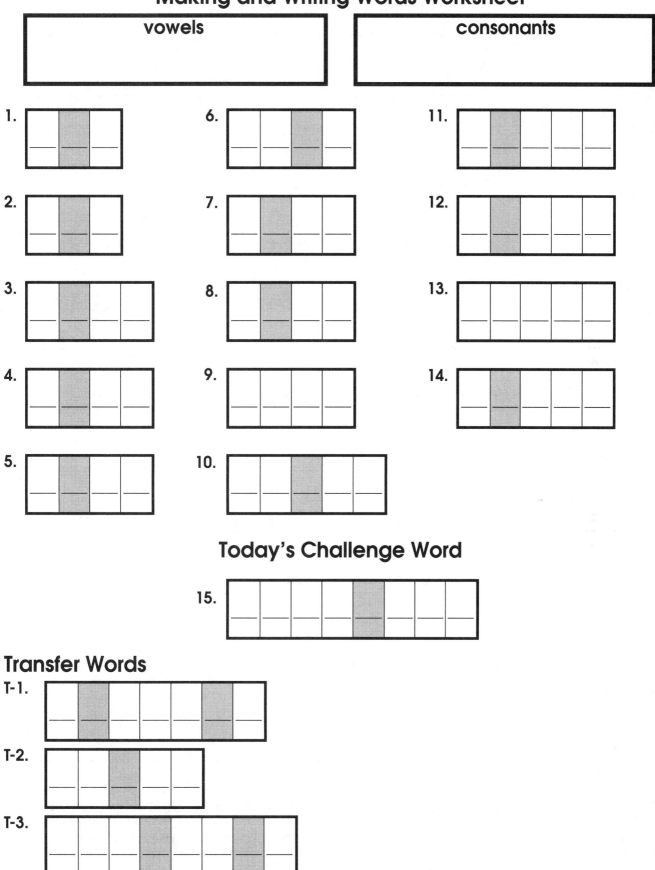

1.

2.

3.

4.

5.

6.

7.

8.

9.

10.

11.

12.

13.

14.

Today's Challenge Word

15.

Transfer Words

T-1.

T-2.

T-3.

85

Making and Writing Words Lesson
Challenge Word: violence

vowels	consonants
e, e, i, o	**c, l, n, v**

Making Words

	Words	Sentence Clue
1.	coil	I wound the extension cord into a coil.
2.	coin	A dime is a small coin that is worth ten cents.
3.	cove	The boat was hidden in the cove away from the pirates.
4.	Vince	I have a cousin whose name is Vince.
5.	vein	Every vein in your body has blood flowing through it.
6.	vice	The vice president gave a speech to the senators.
7.	voice	Jill has a very beautiful voice.
8.	novel	The author wrote an award-winning mystery novel.
9.	olive	I placed a large black olive on top of my salad.
10.	niece	My mom's niece is my cousin.
11.	liven	Listening to music will always liven up a boring day.
12.	clove	My mom put a garlic clove into the chicken soup.
13.	clone	My little brother looks like a clone of my dad.
14.	novice	The first year I played football, I was a novice player.
15.	violence	

Sorts:

1, 2, and 3 syllable words; words containing "s" sounds; words that have words within them; words containing the sound "oy"

Transfer Words

	Words	Clue
1.	violin	The violin is a stringed instrument played with a bow.
2.	convince	I tried to convince my sister to watch the movie with me.
3.	nephew	My brother is my uncle's nephew.

Name _____

Making and Writing Words Worksheet

vowels	consonants

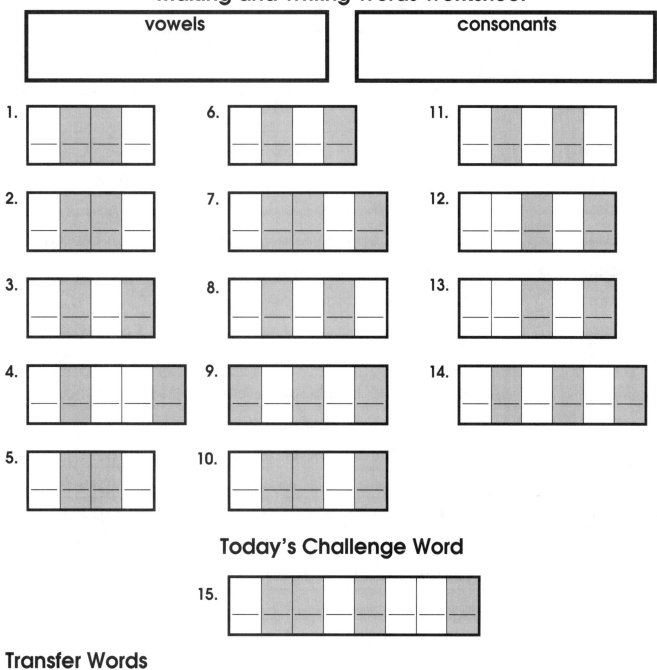

1.

6.

11.

2.

7.

12.

3.

8.

13.

4.

9.

14.

5.

10.

Today's Challenge Word

15.

Transfer Words

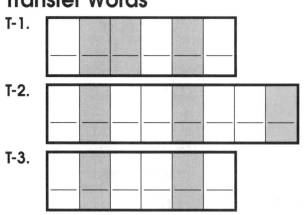

T-1.

T-2.

T-3.

Making and Writing Words Lesson
Challenge Word: yearbook

vowels a, e, o, o	consonants b, k, r, y*

Making Words

	Words	Sentence Clue
1.	okay	Alice's parents said it was okay for her to come visit.
2.	obey	The misbehaving dog would not obey its owners.
3.	bore	I thought the film we were watching was such a bore.
4.	boar	The hunters spotted a wild boar in the woods.
5.	bear	The bear lives in a large cage at the zoo.
6.	bare	His bare arms were sunburned by the end of the day.
7.	beak	The pelican's beak is large enough to hold many fish.
8.	bark	The bark on the tree is rough and covered with moss.
9.	brook	The small brook flowed into a crystal clear lake.
10.	broke	Travis broke his arm when he fell off the swing.
11.	break	She hoped the glass bowl would not break when it fell.
12.	brake	She pressed the brake pedal on her car to stop in time.
13.	baker	The baker created a beautiful cake for my birthday.
14.	bakery	We bought fresh bread from the bakery this afternoon.
15.	yearbook	

Sorts:
words containing "er" sounds; words containing long "o" sounds; words containing long "a" sounds; words that are associated with animals; words that are homophones

Transfer Words

	Words	Clue
1.	broken	The broken window was replaced the very next day.
2.	boring	Our coach's pep talk was anything but boring.
3.	disobey	We are taught not to disobey our parents.

Name _____

Making and Writing Words Worksheet

vowels	consonants

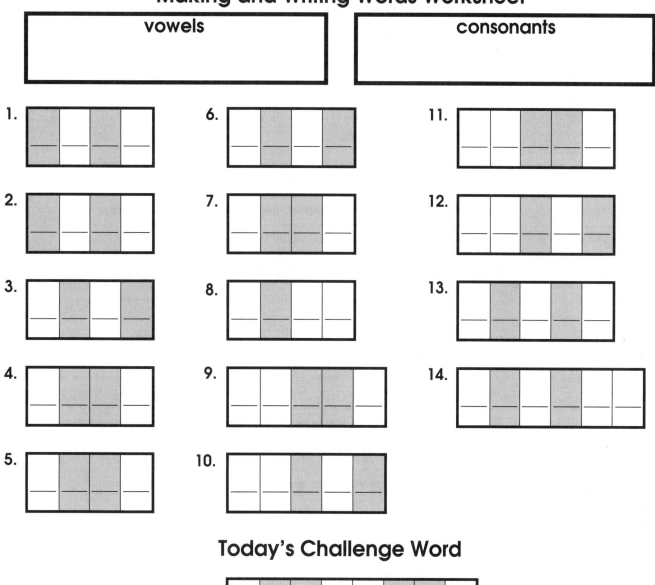

Today's Challenge Word

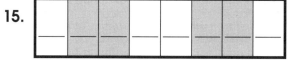

Transfer Words

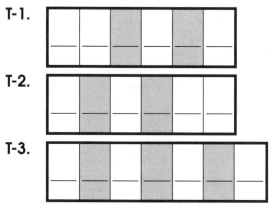

Making and Writing Words Lesson
Challenge Word: apologize

vowels a, e, i, o, o	consonants g, l, p, z

Making Words

	Words	Sentence Clue
1.	pole	The flag pole stands proudly in front of our school.
2.	pale	Kelly looked pale after talking with the principal.
3.	polo	Polo is a game played on horseback.
4.	ooze	The ketchup seemed to ooze slowly out of the bottle.
5.	loop	Loop the rope around the pole before tying the knot.
6.	gaze	I love to gaze up at the stars in the nighttime sky.
7.	goal	My goal is to one day become the president of the U.S.
8.	pool	My mom wants to put a swimming pool in our backyard.
9.	polio	Fortunately, children can be immunized against polio.
10.	igloo	It seems to me that an igloo would not be very warm.
11.	glaze	She put a glaze on her pottery to make it shiny.
12.	agile	Basketball players need to be fast and agile.
13.	goalie	The soccer goalie stopped the other team from scoring.
14.	epilog	The final chapter of the story was a short epilog.
15.	apologize	

Sorts:

1, 2, and 3+ syllable words; words containing long "o" sounds; words containing consonant blends; words containing the "oo" sound; words relating to or used in sports

Transfer Words

	Words	Clue
1.	blaze	Several firefighters were required to extinguish the blaze.
2.	spool	The wire was wound around a large spool.
3.	agility	Stretching exercises can improve a person's agility.

Name _____

Making and Writing Words Worksheet

vowels	consonants

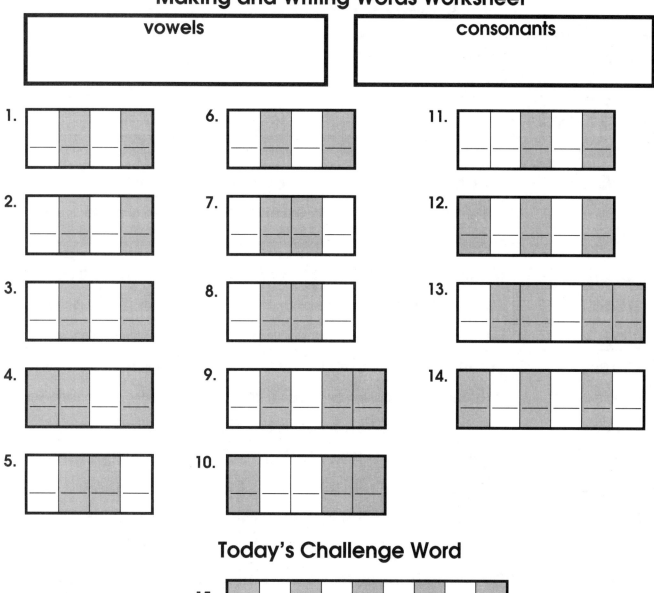

Today's Challenge Word

15.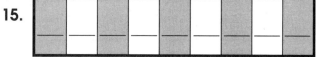

Transfer Words

T-1.
T-2.
T-3.

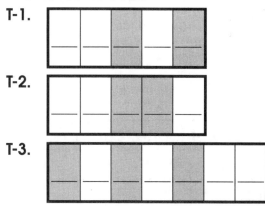

Making and Writing Words Lesson
Challenge Word: architect

vowels **a, e, i**	consonants **c, c, h, r, t, t**

Making Words

Words	Sentence Clue
1. itch	Touching poison ivy may cause you to itch.
2. rich	The miner struck it rich when he discovered gold.
3. arch	The entrance to the old church was a tall marble arch.
4. chart	My first-grade teacher wrote stories on chart paper.
5. reach	Joey hopes to reach six feet tall before he stops growing.
6. teach	I will teach you how to play baseball this afternoon.
7. threat	Some countries are a threat to world peace.
8. tactic	Our team tried a new tactic to score on our opponents.
9. hectic	The last day of school was hectic but exciting.
10. attire	We should wear nice attire to school every day.
11. arctic	The storm was followed by a blast of cold arctic air.
12. ratchet	Dad uses a ratchet wrench when he works on the car.
13. chatter	My teeth began to chatter while I was outside sledding.
14. catcher	The pitcher threw the ball to the catcher at home plate.
15. architect	

Sorts:

1 and 2 syllable words; words containing long vowel sounds; words containing silent letters; words containing "ch" sounds

Transfer Words

Words	Clue
1. charm	My sister received a charm bracelet for her birthday.
2. archer	An archer uses a bow and arrows to compete in his sport.
3. static	Static electricity made my hair stand on end.

Name _____

Making and Writing Words Worksheet

vowels	consonants

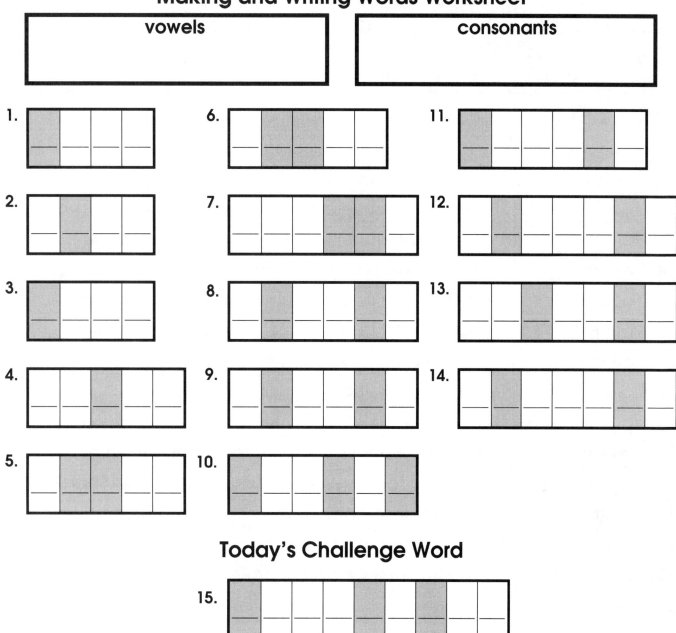

Today's Challenge Word

15.

Transfer Words

T-1.

T-2.

T-3.

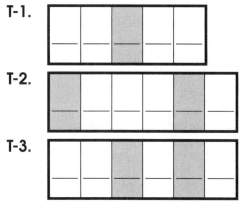

Making and Writing Words Lesson
Challenge Word: cooperate

vowels	consonants
a, e, e, o, o	**c, p, r, t**

Making Words

	Words	Sentence Clue
1.	troop	I belong to a local scout troop.
2.	trace	There was no trace of dirt left after I cleaned my room.
3.	react	How did you react when he crept up behind you?
4.	peace	Most people would prefer peace over war.
5.	opera	Mother likes to listen to opera while she is driving.
6.	crept	The cat silently crept up on the unsuspecting bird.
7.	creep	It is fun to creep up on a friend and surprise her.
8.	crate	The stove came packed in its own crate.
9.	actor	Which actor or actress on that show is your favorite?
10.	repeat	We plan to repeat our performance for the first graders.
11.	create	I would like to create a masterpiece of music or painting.
12.	carpet	We have new carpet on our living room floor.
13.	captor	The captor released the hostages after a few hours.
14.	operate	The doctor said he did not have to operate on my foot.
15.	cooperate	

Sorts:
1, 2, and 3+ syllable words; words containing "ate" sounds; words containing a suffix or prefix; words referring to actions (verbs)

Transfer Words

	Words	Clue
1.	creation	I think that the banana split is a wonderful creation.
2.	operation	The doctor told us that the operation was a success.
3.	reaction	Her reaction to the surprise party was joy and laughter.

94

Name _____

Making and Writing Words Worksheet

vowels	consonants

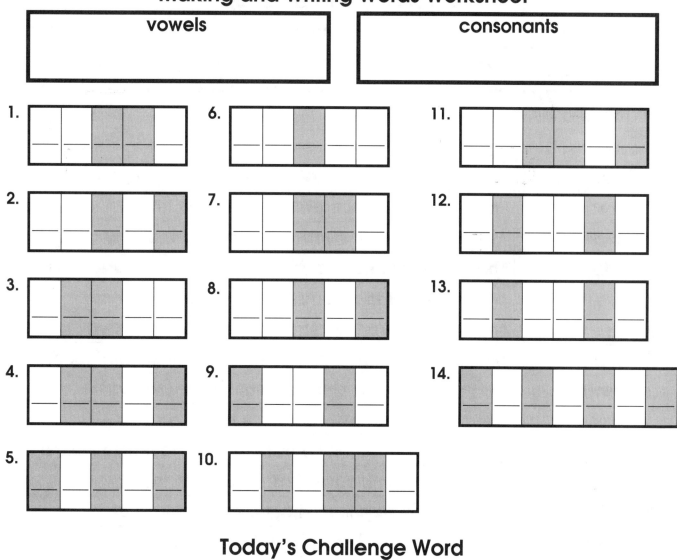

1.
6.
11.

2.
7.
12.

3.
8.
13.

4.
9.
14.

5.
10.

Today's Challenge Word

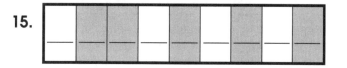

15.

Transfer Words

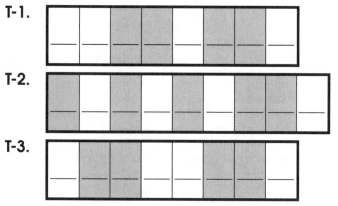

T-1.

T-2.

T-3.

95

Making and Writing Words Lesson
Challenge Word: delicious

vowels e, i, i, o, u	consonants c, d, l, s

Making Words

	Words	Sentence Clue
1.	dose	I have to take a dose of this medicine every six hours.
2.	close	There is a really nice park close to my house.
3.	solid	Matter can take the form of a solid, a liquid, or a gas.
4.	slide	The pool in our neighborhood has a great water slide.
5.	slice	While Mom prepares the bread, I'll slice the ham.
6.	sliced	My father sliced the turkey with a carving knife.
7.	oldies	My favorite songs are the ones I call oldies but goodies.
8.	soiled	The farmer's work clothes were heavily soiled.
9.	docile	The puppy is very docile when he is sleepy.
10.	douse	We had to douse the lights to be able to see the stars.
11.	clouds	I love to watch clouds drifting along in the sky.
12.	coiled	The snake coiled itself around the tree branch.
13.	closed	The restaurant closed promptly at 10:00 last night.
14.	doilies	My grandmother is an expert at making lace doilies.
15.	delicious	

Sorts:
1, 2, and 3+ syllable words; words containing diphthongs; words referring to actions (verbs); words containing long "o" sounds

Transfer Words

	Words	Clue
1.	recoiled	I recoiled at the thought of eating liver one more time.
2.	closest	My closest friend lives just around the corner from me.
3.	closet	My closet is filled with toys, puzzles, and games.

Name _____

Making and Writing Words Worksheet

vowels	consonants

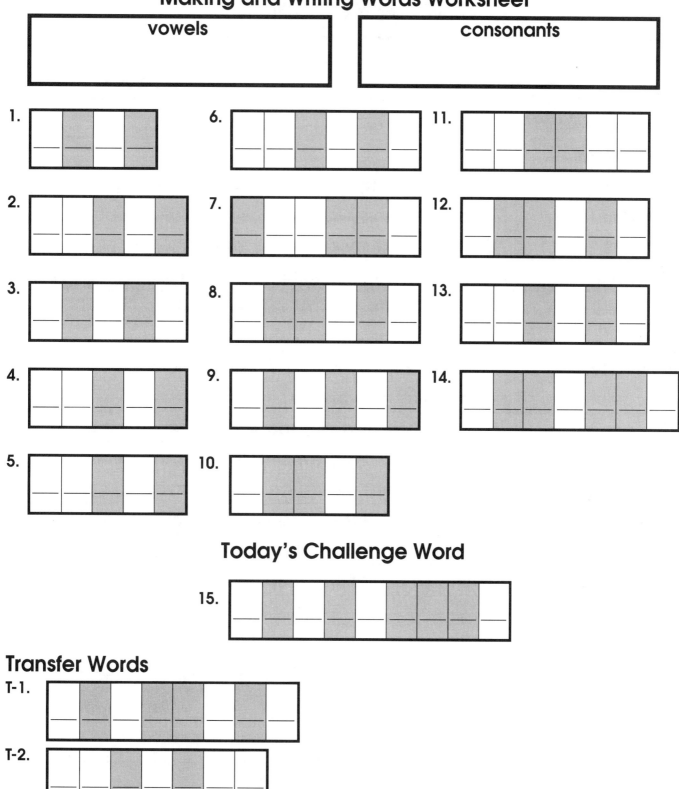

1.

2.

3.

4.

5.

6.

7.

8.

9.

10.

11.

12.

13.

14.

Today's Challenge Word

15.

Transfer Words

T-1.

T-2.

T-3.

Making and Writing Words Lesson
Challenge Word: equipment

vowels e, e, i, u	consonants m, n, p, q, t

Making Words

	Words	Sentence Clue
1.	meet	I always meet my brother at the bus after school.
2.	quit	My father quit his job in order to start his own business.
3.	pint	I drank a pint of milk at lunch today.
4.	punt	On fourth down, the football team had to punt the ball.
5.	untie	I could not untie the knot in the kite string.
6.	unite	We will unite to fight our common enemy.
7.	quite	I thought that the mayor was quite nice when I met him.
8.	quiet	My dad is usually a quiet person.
9.	queen	My sister often acts as if she were queen of the house.
10.	input	My friends ask for my input before making decisions.
11.	inept	I am pretty inept when it comes to playing sports.
12.	equip	The Air Force plans to equip the jet with extra fuel tanks.
13.	minute	Can you hold your breath for one whole minute?
14.	minuet	The minuet was once a popular dance.
15.	equipment	

Sorts:
words containing short "i" sounds; words containing long "i" sounds; words containing short "e" sounds; words containing consonant blends

Transfer Words

	Words	Clue
1.	quilt	I wrapped the quilt around my shoulders to keep warm.
2.	quest	Our class is on a quest for knowledge.
3.	reunited	The lost child was quickly reunited with his mother.

Name _____

Making and Writing Words Worksheet

vowels	consonants

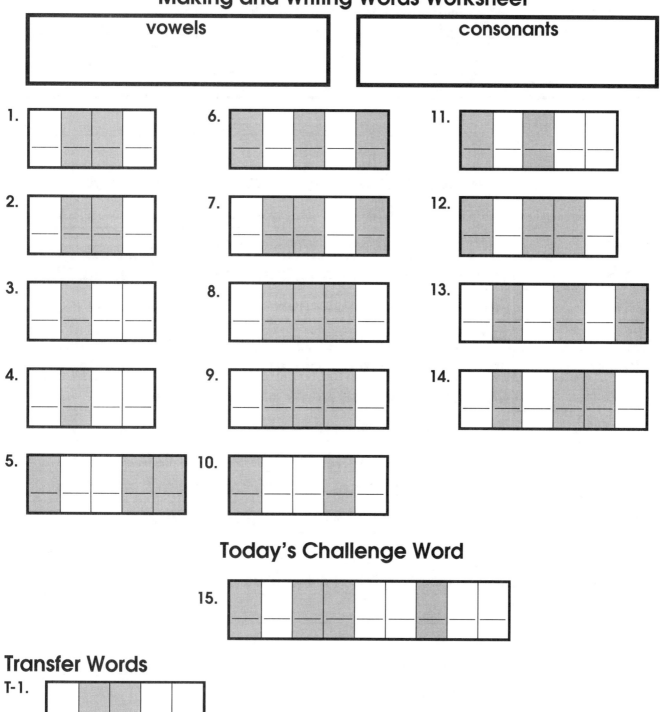

1.

2.

3.

4.

5.

6.

7.

8.

9.

10.

11.

12.

13.

14.

Today's Challenge Word

15.

Transfer Words

T-1.

T-2.

T-3.

99

Making and Writing Words Lesson
Challenge Word: exhibitor

vowels	consonants
e, i, i, o	**b, h, r, t, x**

Making Words

	Words	Sentence Clue
1.	herb	Rosemary is an herb that adds flavor to many dishes.
2.	exit	The red exit sign over the door was blinking on and off.
3.	both	Both of those small brown dogs are beagles.
4.	bite	Beware of strange dogs; they may try to bite you.
5.	tribe	The African tribe was known for its beautiful artwork.
6.	throb	My sore arm continued to throb even after I put ice on it.
7.	their	Their coats are in the closet in the hall.
8.	other	Only one other boy in my class has blonde hair.
9.	orbit	Earth is in orbit around the sun.
10.	broth	My favorite part of chicken noodle soup is the broth.
11.	boxer	The untrained boxer was knocked out in the first round.
12.	birth	My neighbor gave birth to twins last night.
13.	exhibit	Our class went to see a photo exhibit at the art museum.
14.	bother	Bees really bother me because they buzz and sting.
15.	exhibitor	

Sorts:

1, 2, and 3 syllable words; words containing "er" sounds; words containing short "i" sounds; words that have words within them

Transfer Words

	Words	Clue
1.	there	A note for you is over there on the table.
2.	brother	My dad's brother does not look like him at all.
3.	exhibition	The museum put on an exhibition of the artist's paintings.

Name _____

Making and Writing Words Worksheet

vowels	consonants

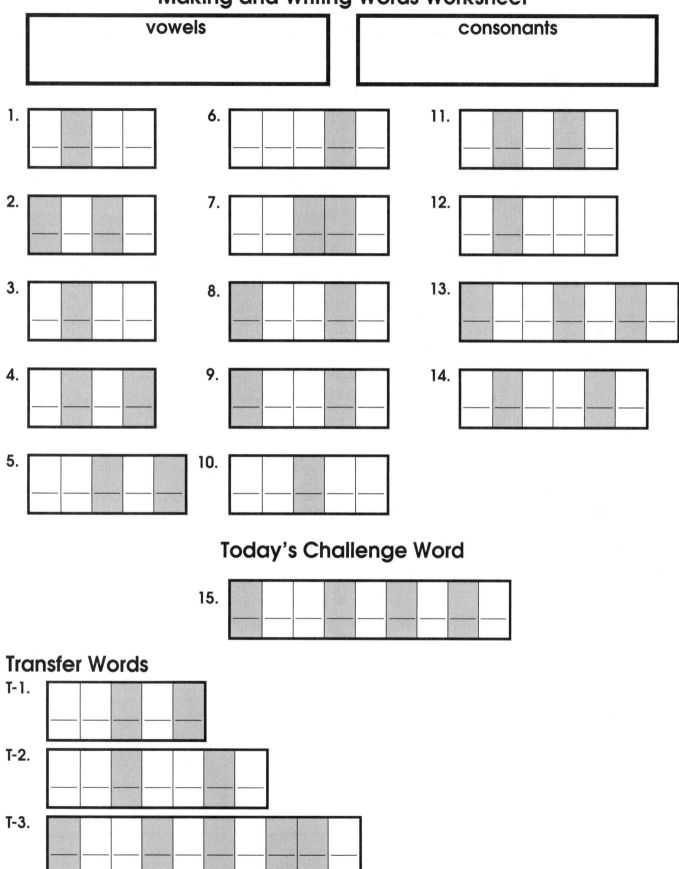

1.

2.

3.

4.

5.

6.

7.

8.

9.

10.

11.

12.

13.

14.

Today's Challenge Word

15.

Transfer Words

T-1.

T-2.

T-3.

Making and Writing Words Lesson
Challenge Word: furniture

vowels	consonants
e, i, u, u	f, n, r, r, t

Making Words

	Words	Sentence Clue
1.	unit	We just completed our Social Studies unit on explorers.
2.	unite	Workers often unite to form labor unions.
3.	untie	I have to untie my shoes to take them off.
4.	unfit	The unfit player was very slow when he ran.
5.	truer	My cousin is a truer friend than my own sister.
6.	tuner	The piano tuner made our piano sound just right.
7.	refit	The ship has to be refit with supplies for its next voyage.
8.	rerun	Tonight's television show is another rerun.
9.	inert	Helium is safe because it is an inert, or inactive, gas.
10.	fruit	Oranges and bananas are my favorite types of fruit.
11.	finer	Silk is a finer cloth than cotton.
12.	return	I plan to return the defective clock to the store.
13.	future	In the future, we may be able to vacation on the moon.
14.	nurture	Mother birds nurture their young until they are able to fly.
15.	furniture	

Sorts:
words containing "er" sounds; words containing long "u" sounds; words containing suffixes or inflected endings; words containing prefixes

Transfer Words

	Words	Clue
1.	reunite	The zookeeper will reunite the bear cub with its mother.
2.	finest	The finest restaurants are usually the most expensive, too.
3.	returnable	Some soda bottles are returnable for a money deposit.

Name _____

Making and Writing Words Worksheet

vowels	consonants

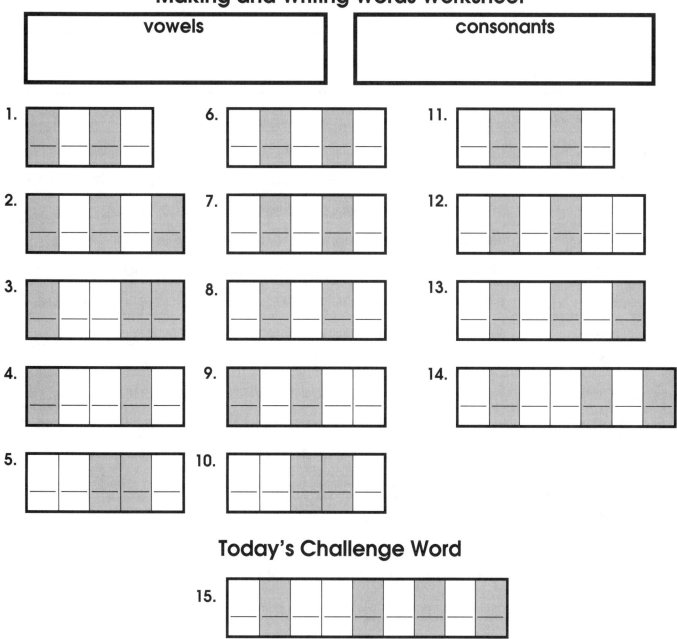

1. 6. 11.

2. 7. 12.

3. 8. 13.

4. 9. 14.

5. 10.

Today's Challenge Word

15.

Transfer Words

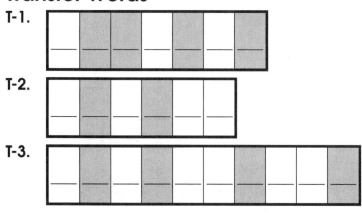

T-1.

T-2.

T-3.

Making and Writing Words Lesson
Challenge Word: guarantee

vowels	consonants
a, a, e, e, u	g, n, r, t

Making Words

	Words	Sentence Clue
1.	grant	I hope Mom will grant me permission to go to the party.
2.	green	The grass seems especially green in the spring.
3.	greet	The hostess stood in the doorway to greet her guests.
4.	great	The high school across town has a great football team.
5.	earn	I hope to earn enough money to buy a new skateboard.
6.	turn	We had to turn around because I forgot my bookbag.
7.	range	We practiced hitting golf balls at the driving range.
8.	urgent	I received an urgent call saying my brother was sick.
9.	tenure	The professor earned tenure after teaching for five years.
10.	neuter	We plan to neuter our dog before he turns one year old.
11.	neater	My bedroom is neater than it was before I cleaned up.
12.	nature	Plants and animals are all part of nature.
13.	garnet	A garnet is a red, semiprecious stone.
14.	enrage	Poor service at a restaurant may enrage the customers.
15.	guarantee	

Sorts:

1, 2, and 3 syllable words; words containing long "e" sounds; words containing long "a" sounds; words that have words within them

Transfer Words

	Words	Clue
1.	urgency	I worked on the special project with a sense of urgency.
2.	engage	The car will not move until the gears engage.
3.	greenery	Our yard has a lot of beautiful greenery around it.

Name _____

Making and Writing Words Worksheet

vowels	consonants

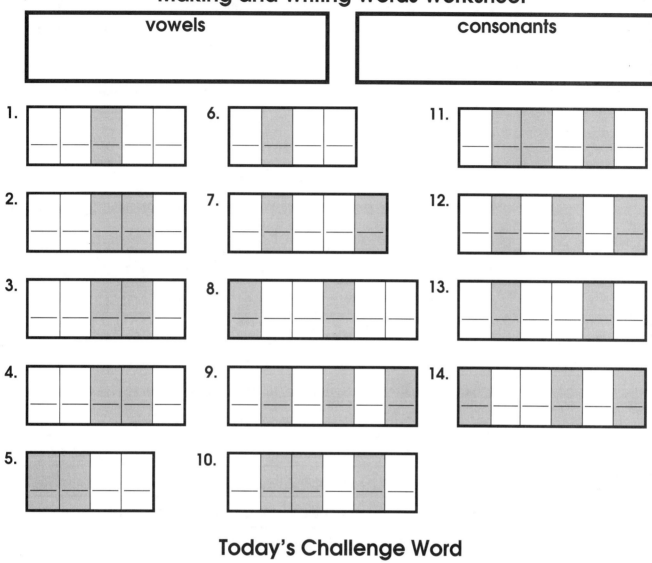

1.
2.
3.
4.
5.
6.
7.
8.
9.
10.
11.
12.
13.
14.

Today's Challenge Word

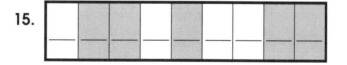

15.

Transfer Words

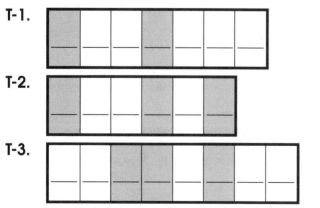

T-1.

T-2.

T-3.

Making and Writing Words Lesson
Challenge Word: hurricane

vowels	consonants
a, e, i, u	**c, h, n, r, r**

Making Words

	Words	Sentence Clue
1.	care	I care a lot about my friends and family.
2.	ache	Noise from the construction site made my head ache.
3.	rain	I hope that the rain will not cancel tomorrow's parade.
4.	ruin	I hope the grape juice I spilled will not ruin the carpet.
5.	ranch	My grandfather owns a cattle ranch in Montana.
6.	chain	The heavy chain across the driveway blocked our path.
7.	crane	The workers used a crane to lift the concrete slabs.
8.	churn	In the old days, people had to churn their own butter.
9.	urchin	The sea urchin is a small marine animal.
10.	richer	When Lisa found the dime, she became ten cents richer.
11.	enrich	Fertilizer helps to enrich the soil.
12.	archer	Someone who uses a bow and arrows is called an archer.
13.	achier	I feel achier today than I did yesterday.
14.	rancher	The rancher owns over one hundred head of cattle.
15.	hurricane	

Sorts:
1, 2, and 3 syllable words; words containing "er" sounds; words containing long "a" sounds; words containing "ich" sounds; words that are related to each other

Transfer Words

	Words	Clue
1.	enriched	We were enriched by the experience of seeing the play.
2.	richest	Mr. Potter is said to be the richest man in town.
3.	church	That church was built over two hundred years ago.

Name _____

Making and Writing Words Worksheet

vowels	consonants

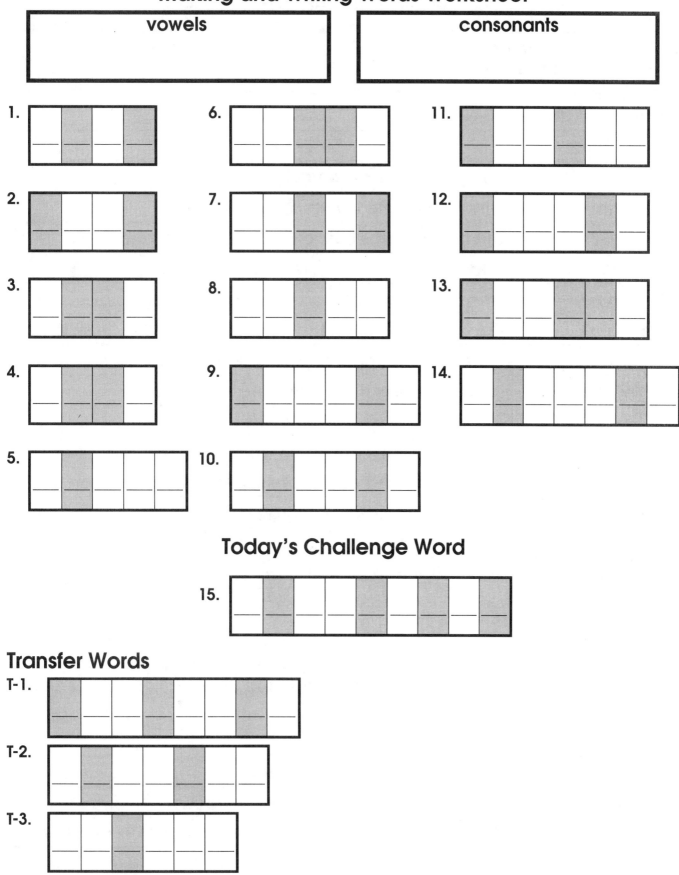

Today's Challenge Word

15.

Transfer Words

T-1.

T-2.

T-3.

Making and Writing Words Lesson
Challenge Word: satellite

vowels	consonants
a, e, e, i	**l, l, s, t, t**

Making Words

	Words	Sentence Clue
1.	tale	Cinderella was my favorite fairy tale as a child.
2.	steal	It is wrong to steal from another person.
3.	steel	The building was built out of steel, glass, and brick.
4.	tells	I like it when Grandpa tells us funny stories.
5.	stale	Bread that is left out too long gets hard and stale.
6.	slate	The walkway through the garden was paved with slate tiles.
7.	title	I am thinking about a good title for my story.
8.	settle	I hope my new puppy will settle down soon.
9.	little	The little boy held his mother's hand tightly.
10.	latest	The latest I can stay up on a school night is 9:00 p.m.
11.	titles	Look in the card catalog to find the book titles you need.
12.	estate	The estate consists of a large home on five acres of land.
13.	allies	The allies worked together to win the war.
14.	tallest	Rachel is the tallest girl in my class.
15.	satellite	

Sorts:

1, 2, and 3 syllable words; words containing long vowel sounds; words containing double letters; words describing superlative relationships (ending in "est")

Transfer Words

	Words	Clue
1.	littlest	Katie is the littlest girl on the playground.
2.	stalest	This is the hardest and stalest bread I have ever eaten.
3.	settlement	The pioneers created a settlement near the river.

Name _____

Making and Writing Words Worksheet

vowels	consonants

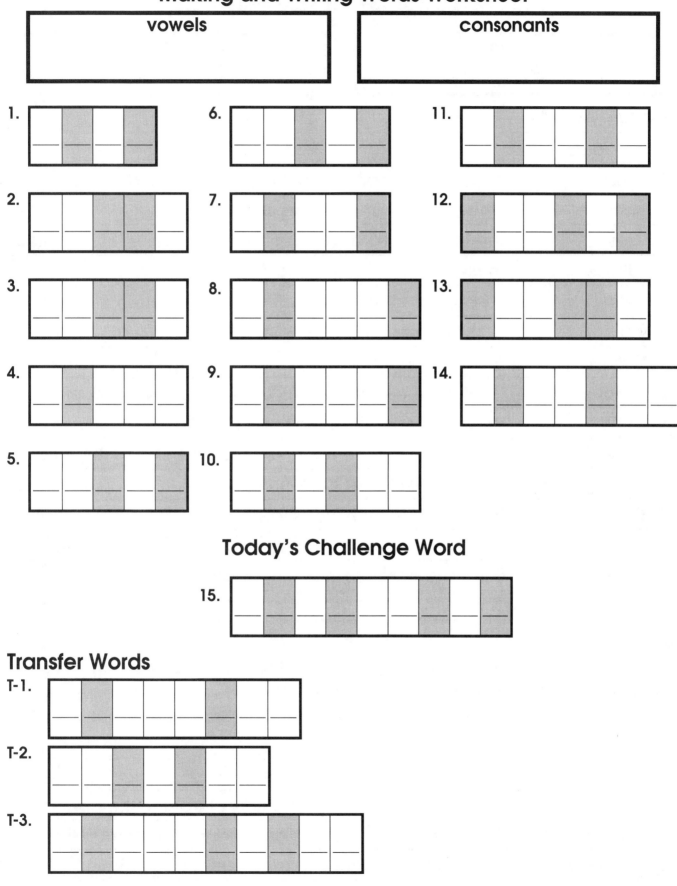

1.

2.

3.

4.

5.

6.

7.

8.

9.

10.

11.

12.

13.

14.

Today's Challenge Word

15.

Transfer Words

T-1.

T-2.

T-3.

Making and Writing Words Lesson
Challenge Word: southwest

vowels	consonants
e, o, u	**h, s, s, t, t, w**

Making Words

	Words	Sentence Clue
1.	toss	If you toss the ball into the hoop, you will score two points.
2.	whose	Whose pencil is this on the table?
3.	tests	The tests were graded and handed back to the students.
4.	those	Those books over there belong to me.
5.	stews	My mom makes the best soups and stews.
6.	south	Florida is located to the south of Georgia.
7.	shots	The hockey player took three shots during the game.
8.	shoes	I tied my shoes, put on my coat, and left for school.
9.	hosts	The hosts welcomed me to their party.
10.	hoses	We connected two hoses to reach the end of the yard.
11.	shout	I had to shout over the loud music.
12.	stout	The stout little man was shorter than me.
13.	outset	From the outset, I knew that we could win the game.
14.	houses	Our houses are located on the same street.
15.	southwest	

Sorts:

1 and 2 syllable words; words containing the "ou" sound; words that have words within them; words that are plural

Transfer Words

	Words	Clue
1.	southeast	We drove southeast for two hours to get to the city.
2.	shouted	I shouted at my teammates to keep up the good work.
3.	hostess	Lisa was the hostess of a great birthday party.

Name _____

Making and Writing Words Worksheet

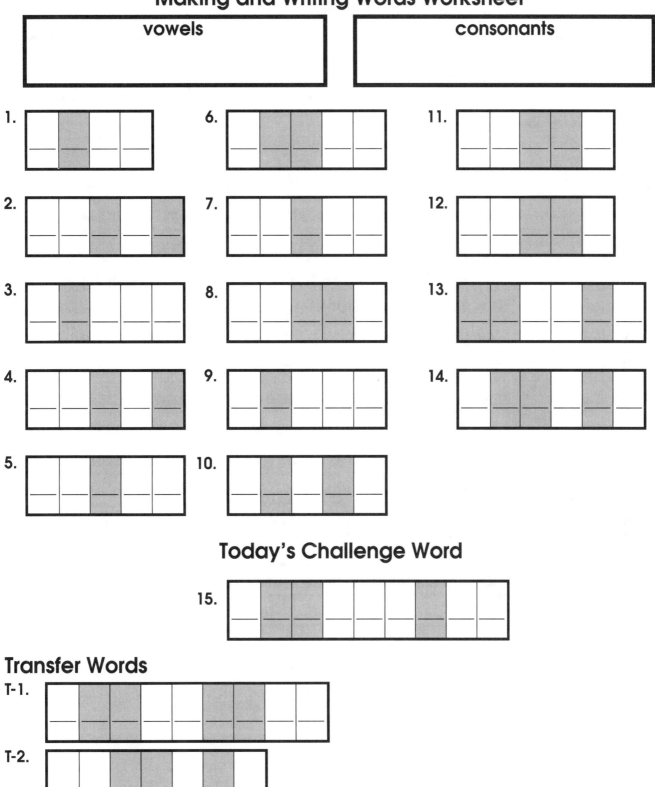

| vowels | consonants |

1.
2.
3.
4.
5.
6.
7.
8.
9.
10.
11.
12.
13.
14.

Today's Challenge Word

15.

Transfer Words

T-1.

T-2.

T-3.

Making and Writing Words Lesson
Challenge Word: technique

vowels	consonants
e, e, i, u	**c, h, n, q, t**

Making Words

Words	Sentence Clue
1. then	First I will do my homework, then I will call my best friend.
2. thin	The bread was sliced thin for making sandwiches.
3. untie	Charlie tried to untie his shoelaces very quickly.
4. unite	The politician tried to unite the people behind his cause.
5. quiet	It was so quiet, I could hear leaves rustling in the breeze.
6. quite	My parents are quite proud of my accomplishments.
7. queen	The queen bee is larger than all the others in the hive.
8. niece	I took my niece and nephew to the movies last night.
9. hence	We won the game; hence, we were awarded the trophy.
10. chute	We rode the twisting water chute at the amusement park.
11. ethic	Fighting goes against the ethic of kindness to all people.
12. ethnic	There are many different ethnic groups in the world.
13. entice	The idea of dessert could entice me to clean my plate.
14. quench	I drank a lot of water to quench my thirst.
15. technique	

Sorts:
words containing long "i" sounds; words containing "kw" sounds; words containing consonant digraphs; words containing silent letters

Transfer Words

Words	Clue
1. require	Going to college will require a great deal of hard work.
2. enticing	The buried gold was enticing to all the treasure hunters.
3. uniting	It is nice to see people uniting to celebrate school spirit.

Name _____

Making and Writing Words Worksheet

vowels	consonants

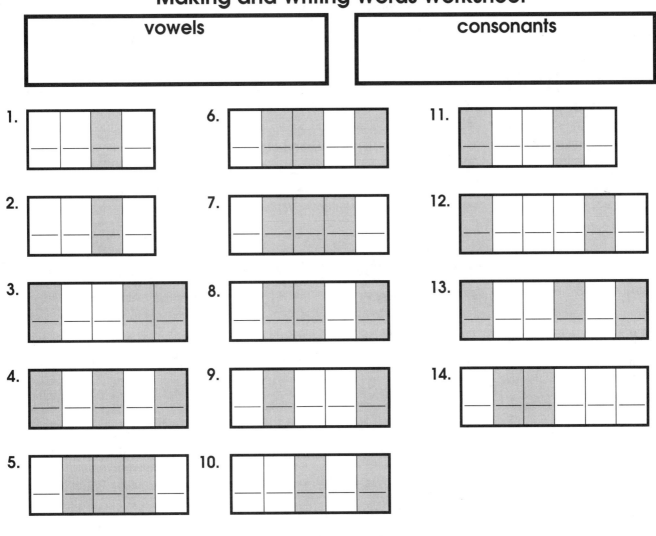

1.

6.

11.

2.

7.

12.

3.

8.

13.

4.

9.

14.

5.

10.

Today's Challenge Word

15.

Transfer Words

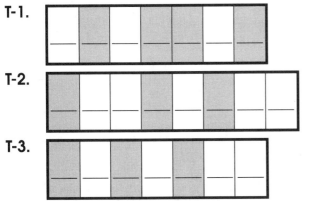

T-1.

T-2.

T-3.

Making and Writing Words Lesson
Challenge Word: telephone

vowels	consonants
e, e, e, o	**h, l, n, p, t**

Making Words

	Words	Sentence Clue
1.	open	I will open the window to let in some fresh air.
2.	poet	The poet has a special way with words.
3.	pelt	The beaver pelt was worth a lot to the fur traders.
4.	peel	I asked my mother to peel the banana for me.
5.	note	Mom gave me a note to give to my teacher.
6.	lent	Yesterday, I lent my sister a brown sweater.
7.	tone	The tone of her voice let me know that Meredith was sad.
8.	lone	The lone survivor of the contest was declared the winner.
9.	hope	I hope that I will get a dog for my birthday.
10.	hole	We dug a hole in the yard for the new plant Mom bought.
11.	help	I will help my mom by drying the dishes.
12.	heel	My heel hurts after running two miles.
13.	phone	I will phone my grandparents to tell them I love them.
14.	hotel	We will stay in a hotel when we go on our trip.
15.	telephone	

Sorts:

words containing "el" sounds; words containing long "o" sounds; words containing long "e" sounds

Transfer Words

	Words	Clue
1.	lend	I lend my sister money all the time.
2.	opener	The can opener is on the kitchen counter.
3.	helpful	My sister is very helpful when it comes to giving advice.

Name _____

Making and Writing Words Worksheet

vowels	consonants

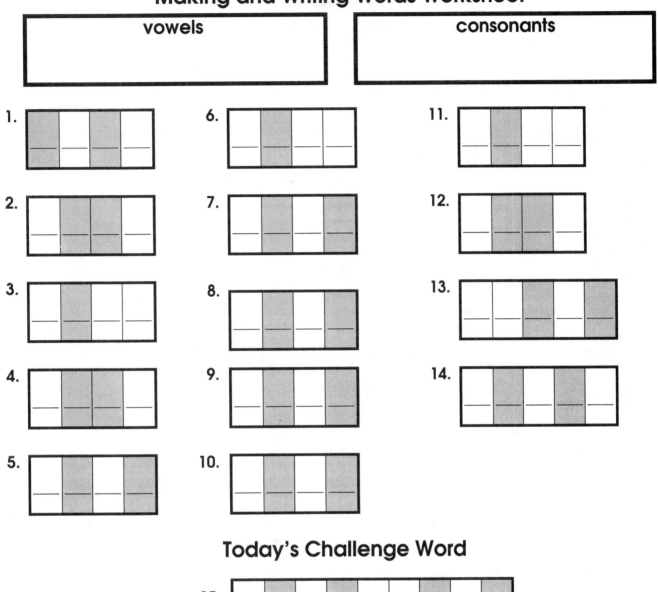

1.   6.   11.

2.   7.   12.

3.   8.   13.

4.   9.   14.

5.   10.

Today's Challenge Word

15.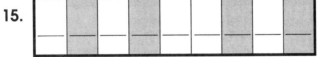

Transfer Words

T-1.

T-2.

T-3.

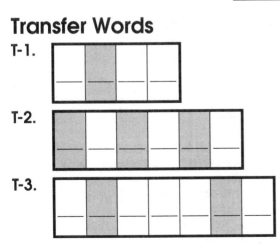

Making and Writing Words Lesson
Challenge Word: telescope

vowels	consonants
e, e, e, o	**c, l, p, s, t**

Making Words

	Words	Sentence Clue
1.	pest	My little brother can be such a pest.
2.	pelt	A thunderstorm could pelt the area with huge raindrops.
3.	lose	I do not want to lose tonight's game.
4.	pole	The basketball hoop is set on top of a ten foot pole.
5.	peel	I prefer to peel the skin off an apple before I eat it.
6.	seep	Water began to seep under the door during the flood.
7.	sleep	Everyone needs around eight hours of sleep each night.
8.	sleet	The sleet and freezing rain eventually turned to snow.
9.	slope	The hill in the park is a great slope for sledding.
10.	scope	The scope of the problem is larger than we had thought.
11.	elect	Who do you think we should elect as class president?
12.	select	Emily prefers to select her own clothes to wear to school.
13.	closet	My closet is filled with shirts and pants.
14.	steeple	The church bell is located high up in the steeple.
15.	telescope	

Sorts:

1, 2, and 3 syllable words; words containing a silent "e"; words containing long "e" sounds; words containing long "o" sounds; words that have words within them

Transfer Words

	Words	Clue
1.	microscope	Today we looked at tiny cells through a microscope.
2.	election	The candidate made many promises before the election.
3.	selection	I considered my choices before making my selection.

Name _____

Making and Writing Words Worksheet

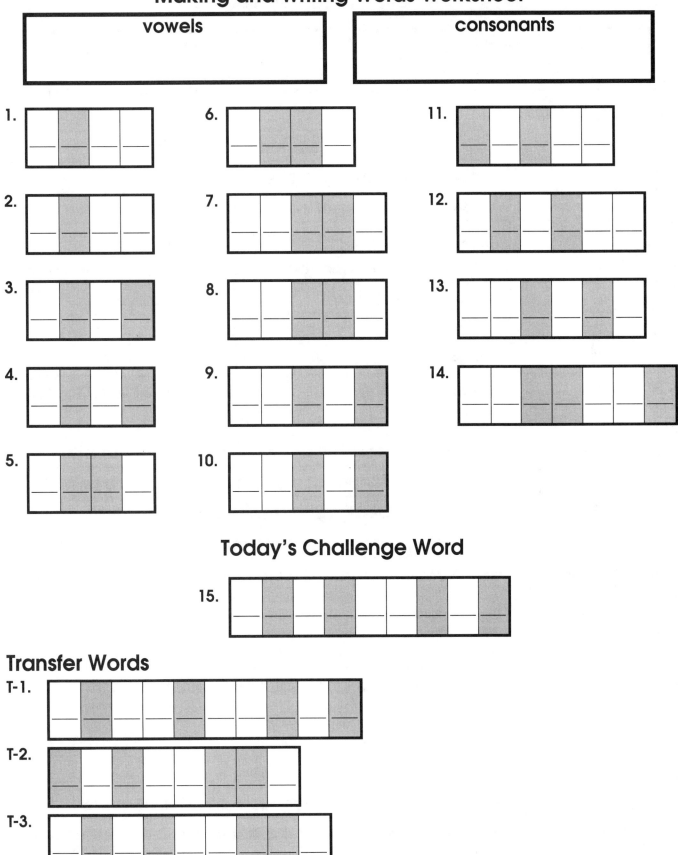

| vowels | consonants |

1.

2.

3.

4.

5.

6.

7.

8.

9.

10.

11.

12.

13.

14.

Today's Challenge Word

15.

Transfer Words

T-1.

T-2.

T-3.

117

Making and Writing Words Lesson
Challenge Word: volunteer

vowels	consonants
e, e, o, u	**l, n, r, t, v**

Making Words

	Words	Sentence Clue
1.	love	I know my parents love me very much.
2.	volt	A volt is a measure of electrical force.
3.	lover	The dog lover spoiled her new puppy with a lot of toys.
4.	loner	He was called a loner because he liked to be by himself.
5.	rove	My dog loves to rove in forests and meadows.
6.	overt	He made his opinions known through his overt statements.
7.	vent	The vent helped air circulate through the house.
8.	event	The play was the one event that no one wanted to miss.
9.	lure	The hunter tried to lure the bear closer to his traps.
10.	teen	Teen girls like to listen to music and talk on the phone.
11.	tenure	A president's tenure can be no more than two terms.
12.	revolt	The colonists decided to revolt against the king.
13.	relent	I hope my parents will relent and let me see the movie.
14.	venture	We hope our business venture is successful and profitable.
15.	volunteer	

Sorts:

1, 2, and 3 syllable words; words containing "er" sounds; words containing long "o" sounds; words containing long "e" sounds; words describing people

Transfer Words

	Words	Clue
1.	relentless	Louis grew tired of his parents' relentless nagging.
2.	lunar	Lisa and Jack looked at the sky to see the lunar eclipse.
3.	inventor	Thomas Edison is the inventor of the first electric light.

Making and Writing Words Worksheet

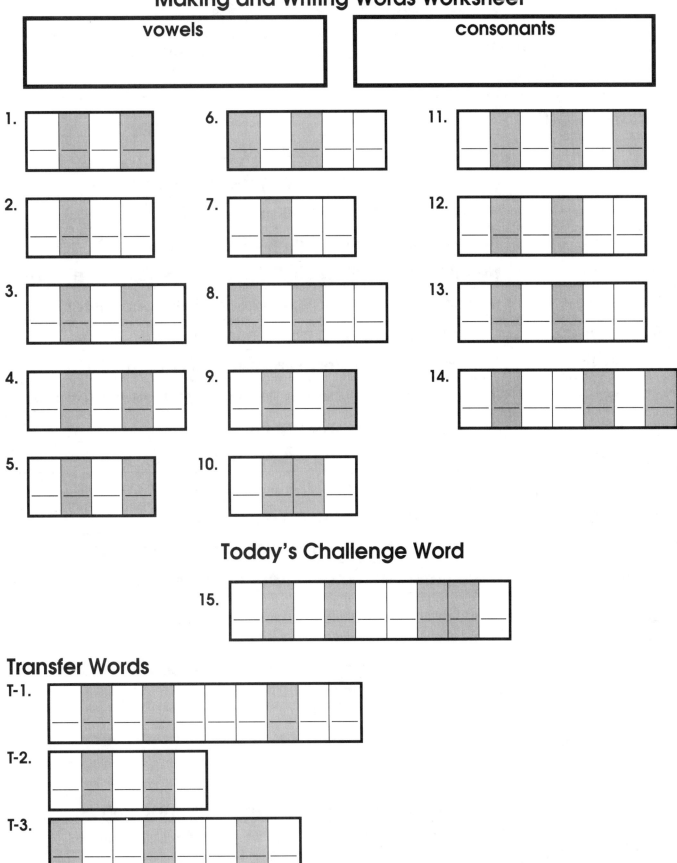

vowels	consonants

1.
2.
3.
4.
5.
6.
7.
8.
9.
10.
11.
12.
13.
14.

Today's Challenge Word

15.

Transfer Words

T-1.

T-2.

T-3.

Making and Writing Words Lesson
Challenge Word: hemisphere

vowels	consonants
e, e, e, i	**h, h, m, p, r, s**

Making Words

	Words	Sentence Clue
1.	sheep	The shepherd guided the sheep into the pen.
2.	prim	We looked very prim and proper for the wedding.
3.	prism	The prism separated the light into a rainbow of colors.
4.	prime	We all tuned in to watch the prime time television show.
5.	piers	We fished from several piers along the ocean front.
6.	peers	I like to hang out with my peers on the weekend.
7.	miser	The old miser was very stingy with his money.
8.	heirs	Those children will be the heirs to their parents' fortune.
9.	eerie	That eerie movie gave me the creeps.
10.	sphere	Earth is a planet in the shape of a sphere.
11.	shrimp	We ordered shrimp at the seafood restaurant.
12.	empire	The great leader ruled his empire wisely.
13.	premise	The premise of the movie was not very believable.
14.	empires	There have been many great empires throughout history.
15.	hemisphere	

Sorts:
words containing "sh" sounds; words containing long "e" sounds; words referring to people; words containing consonant blends

Transfer Words

	Words	Clue
1.	sheepish	The embarassed boy gave me a sheepish grin.
2.	spherical	The deflated basketball lost its spherical shape.
3.	empress	The empress ruled over the land for 50 years.

Name _____

Making and Writing Words Worksheet

vowels	consonants

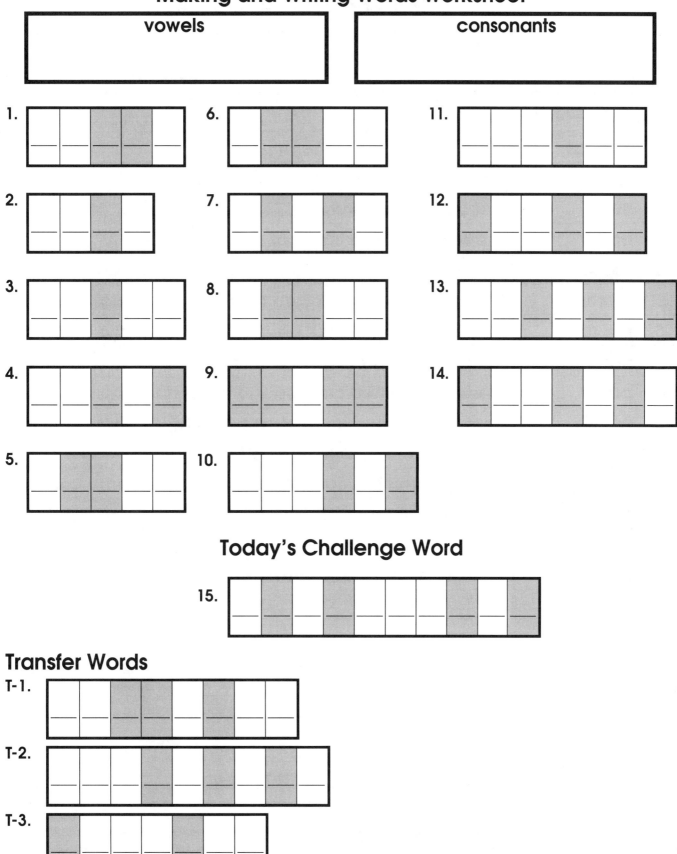

1.

6.

11.

2.

7.

12.

3.

8.

13.

4.

9.

14.

5.

10.

Today's Challenge Word

15.

Transfer Words

T-1.

T-2.

T-3.

Making and Writing Words Lesson
Challenge Word: predator

vowels	consonants
a, e, o	**d, p, r, r, t**

Making Words

Words	Sentence Clue
1. read	You will become smarter if you read a lot of books.
2. tread	Laura can tread water for almost five minutes at a time.
3. trader	A stockbroker is a trader of stocks and bonds.
4. tarred	We tarred the roof in order to stop it from leaking.
5. roared	The lion roared as I walked past him at the zoo.
6. retard	Disinfectants help retard the growth of germs and bacteria.
7. report	I am writing a report about sharks.
8. porter	The porter carried our luggage to our hotel room.
9. parted	The crowd parted to reveal a beautiful Christmas tree.
10. parrot	A parrot is a bird with many brightly colored feathers.
11. deport	A judge ruled to deport the criminal to his home country.
12. depart	The ship will depart for London tomorrow afternoon.
13. adorer	She was known as an adorer of every kind of flower.
14. teardrop	A single teardrop ran down my face.
15. predator	

Sorts:

1, 2, and 3+ syllable words; words containing "or" sounds; words containing prefixes; words that are compound words

Transfer Words

Words	Clue
1. adoration	The cheering crowd displayed its adoration for the hero.
2. airport	Father is going to meet us at the airport today.
3. transportation	A bus is a type of mass transportation.

Name _____

Making and Writing Words Worksheet

vowels	consonants

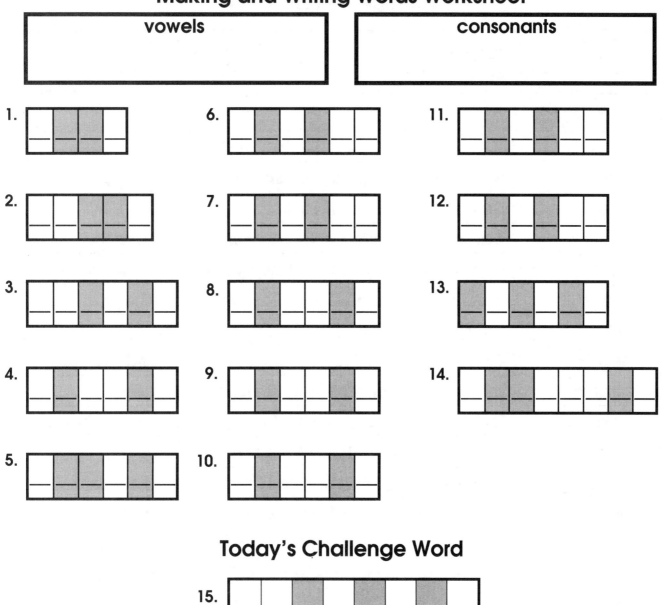

1.
2.
3.
4.
5.
6.
7.
8.
9.
10.
11.
12.
13.
14.

Today's Challenge Word

15.

Transfer Words

T-1.

T-2.

T-3.

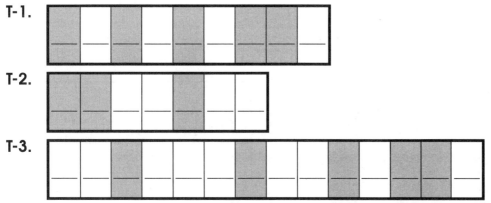

Making and Writing Words Lesson
Challenge Word: theaters

vowels	consonants
a, e, e	**h, r, s, t, t**

Making Words

	Words	Sentence Clue
1.	sheer	Her scarf was made from sheer blue fabric.
2.	three	Delaney has just turned three years old.
3.	tease	Dad said not to tease the dog with table scraps.
4.	taster	Grandma always lets me be the first taster of her cakes.
5.	street	Always look both ways before you cross the street.
6.	setter	An Irish setter is a large, long-haired dog.
7.	hearts	On Valentine's Day, we ate cookies shaped like hearts.
8.	hearse	The hearse carried the coffin to the cemetery.
9.	estate	The millionaire's estate included a large manor house.
10.	earth	Earth is the third planet from the sun.
11.	treats	Mom always packs special treats in my lunch box.
12.	threats	The old man's threats kept us out of his yard.
13.	shatter	I saw the window shatter when the baseball hit it.
14.	heater	We use an electric heater to help keep our house warm.
15.	theaters	

Sorts:
1 and 2 syllable words; words containing long "e" sounds; words containing silent letters

Transfer Words

	Words	Clue
1.	teasing	Mom often tells me to stop teasing the dog.
2.	tasting	I love tasting my mom's home-cooked recipes.
3.	tasty	The orange was tasty and juicy.

Name _____

Making and Writing Words Worksheet

vowels	consonants

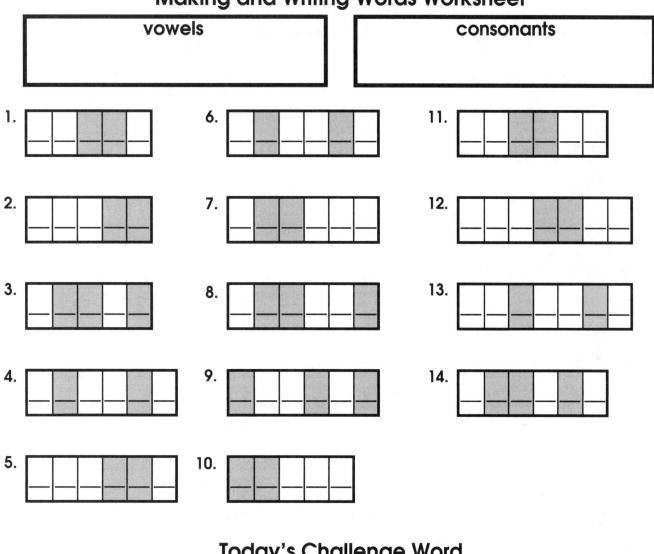

Today's Challenge Word

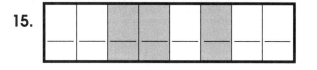

15.

Transfer Words

T-1.

T-2.

T-3.

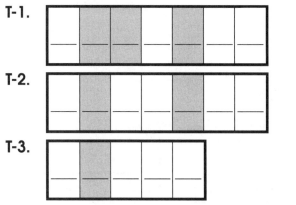

Making and Writing Words Lesson
Challenge Word: adventure

vowels	consonants
a, e, e, u	**d, n, t, r, v**

Making Words

	Words	Sentence Clue
1.	enter	The sign on the old empty house said, "Do not enter."
2.	neater	My sister's room is much neater than mine.
3.	nature	I love to camp in the woods and feel close to nature.
4.	endure	On Friday, we have to endure a very long bus ride.
5.	earned	I earned twenty dollars last week cutting grass.
6.	Avenue	My best friend lives on Jefferson Avenue.
7.	ranted	The drivers ranted about the high cost of gasoline.
8.	advent	The advent of spring is marked by blooming flowers.
9.	veteran	My uncle is a veteran of the Vietnam War.
10.	turned	I turned around quickly when Jamie called my name.
11.	denture	Grandpa uses a denture to replace his missing teeth.
12.	averted	The pilot averted disaster by making a sudden landing.
13.	venture	I will not venture to guess if it will rain tomorrow or not.
14.	ventured	The lost children had ventured too far from home.
15.	adventure	

Sorts:
words containing "er" sounds; words belonging to the "en" word family; words containing a silent letter; words that have words within them

Transfer Words

	Words	Clue
1.	nurture	Parents need to love and nurture their children.
2.	endurance	Running a marathon requires a lot of endurance.
3.	natural	Tony seems to be a natural at playing the trombone.

Name _____

Making and Writing Words Worksheet

vowels	consonants

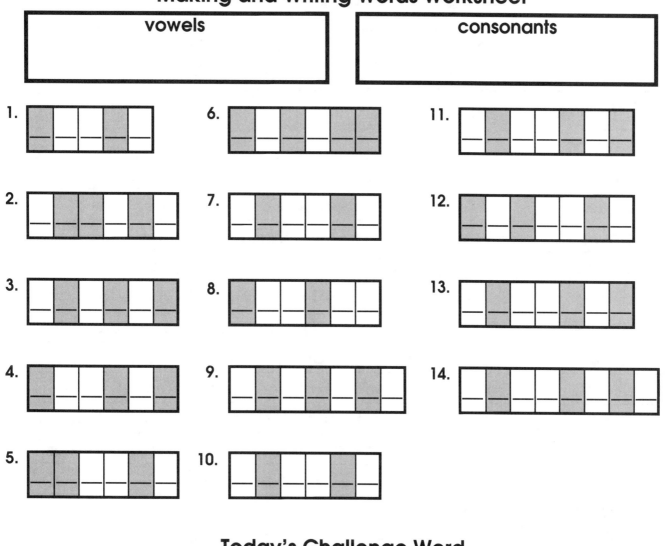

1.
2.
3.
4.
5.

6.
7.
8.
9.
10.

11.
12.
13.
14.

Today's Challenge Word

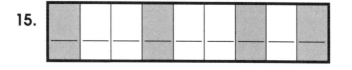

15.

Transfer Words

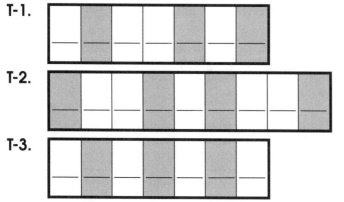

T-1.

T-2.

T-3.

Making and Writing Words Lesson
Challenge Word: advertise

vowels	consonants
a, e, e, i	**d, r, s, t, v**

Making Words

	Words	Sentence Clue
1.	rivet	A rivet was used to hold the pieces of metal together.
2.	trade	It is fun to trade collectible cards with your friends.
3.	starve	If I don't eat soon, I think I will starve.
4.	advise	My parents advise me to do my homework early.
5.	divert	I read a book to divert my attention from the long drive.
6.	diverse	My friends and I all come from diverse backgrounds.
7.	starved	I knew the cat was starved because it ate so fast.
8.	riveted	I was riveted to the exciting book for hours.
9.	revised	I revised my book report after talking with the teacher.
10.	dearest	My dearest possession is my old, ragged teddy bear.
11.	adviser	My dad is my most trusted adviser.
12.	adverse	In adverse weather, I always bring my jacket.
13.	steadier	The table was much steadier after we repaired its legs.
14.	deviate	The coach told us not to deviate from our game plan.
15.	advertise	

Sorts:

1, 2, and 3+ syllable words; words containing long "i" sounds; words containing consonant blends; words that are written in past tense

Transfer Words

	Words	Clue
1.	advertisement	The television advertisement featured a dancing dog.
2.	diversion	Watching movies is a nice diversion from work.
3.	steady	You have to be very steady when walking a tightrope.

Name _____

Making and Writing Words Worksheet

vowels	consonants

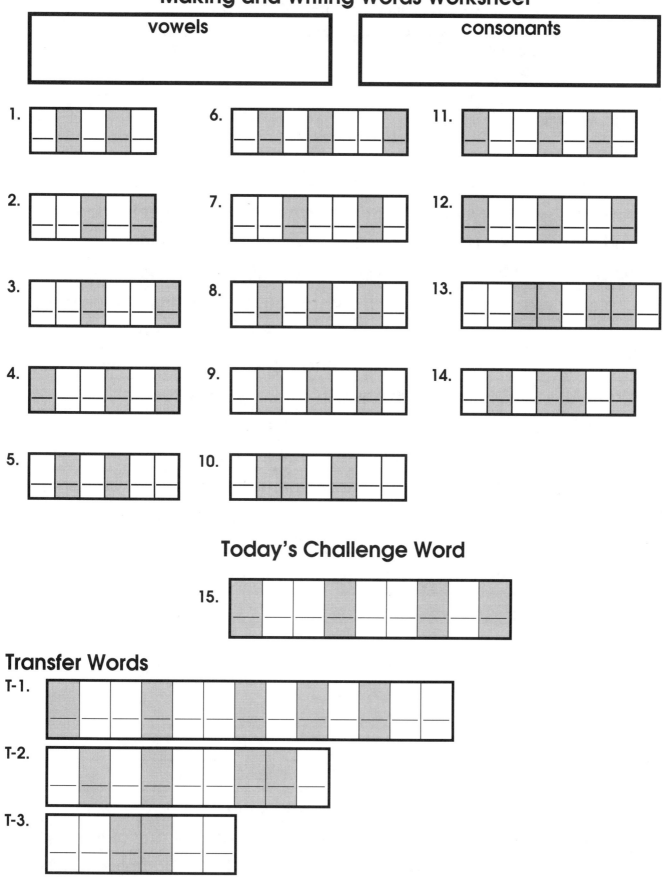

1.

2.

3.

4.

5.

6.

7.

8.

9.

10.

11.

12.

13.

14.

Today's Challenge Word

15.

Transfer Words

T-1.

T-2.

T-3.

Making and Writing Words Lesson
Challenge Word: astounded

vowels	consonants
a, e, o, u	**d, d, n, s, t**

Making Words

	Words	Sentence Clue
1.	sundae	I ordered a hot fudge sundae at the ice cream shop.
2.	sudden	The sudden thunderstorm drenched the neighborhood.
3.	sadden	Rude people sadden me with their behavior.
4.	oddest	We saw the oddest looking airplane at the air show.
5.	dusted	Jamal dusted off his baseball mitt for little league tryouts.
6.	dents	The hailstorm left large dents in the hood of the car.
7.	stand	The firemen asked us to stand aside while they worked.
8.	stone	The log cabin has a large stone fireplace.
9.	snout	The pig has an odd-looking snout.
10.	donuts	Most doughnuts are too sweet for me.
11.	donate	Our family will donate canned food to the food bank.
12.	sounded	Our school band sounded terrific in the parade.
13.	astound	Susan continues to astound me with her many talents.
14.	donated	We donated the clothes to a local charity organization.
15.	astounded	

Sorts:
words containing "ow" sounds (as in "town"); words containing short "u" sounds; words containing double letters

Transfer Words

	Words	Clue
1.	Sunday	Sunday is my favorite day of the week.
2.	saddest	The last day of vacation is the saddest day of the year.
3.	donation	Our class will make a donation to the homeless shelter.

Name _____

Making and Writing Words Worksheet

vowels	consonants

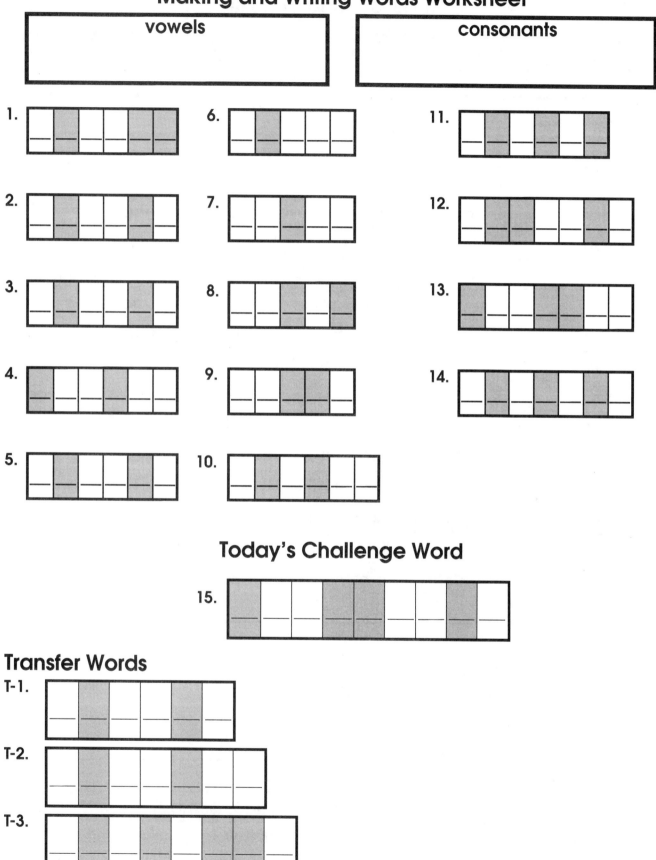

1.

6.

11.

2.

7.

12.

3.

8.

13.

4.

9.

14.

5.

10.

Today's Challenge Word

15.

Transfer Words

T-1.

T-2.

T-3.

131

Making and Writing Words Lesson
Challenge Word: frostbite

vowels	consonants
e, i, o	b, f, r, s, t, t

Making Words

	Words	Sentence Clue
1.	store	I bought this toy at the new discount store.
2.	frost	It was so cold that frost covered all the windows.
3.	fibers	Cotton fibers make the shirt soft and comfortable.
4.	tribes	There are many Native American tribes in the United States.
5.	strife	The disagreement caused a lot of strife among the men.
6.	softer	The softer pillow is more comfortable to me.
7.	bitter	Dark chocolate tastes slightly bitter to me.
8.	sifter	The cook used a sifter to sprinkle flour on the baking pan.
9.	orbits	Earth orbits the Sun in a year's time.
10.	bistro	We ate lunch at a little bistro down the street.
11.	otters	Otters love to play in the water.
12.	foster	Let us try to foster peace throughout the world.
13.	forest	The forest is filled with trees and animals.
14.	forties	Some fashions from the forties are popular again today.
15.	frostbite	

Sorts:

1, 2, and 3 syllable words; words containing "er" sounds; words containing long "i" sounds; words containing short "i" sounds

Transfer Words

	Words	Clue
1.	shore	The ocean waves crashed against the shore.
2.	bitterness	Try not to feel any bitterness toward your enemies.
3.	softness	The softness of the blanket feels good against my skin.

Name _____

Making and Writing Words Worksheet

vowels	consonants

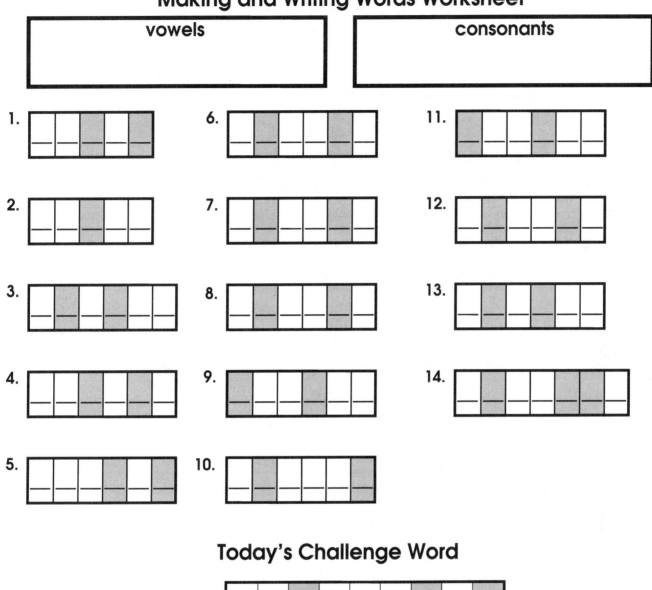

1.
2.
3.
4.
5.
6.
7.
8.
9.
10.
11.
12.
13.
14.

Today's Challenge Word

15.

Transfer Words

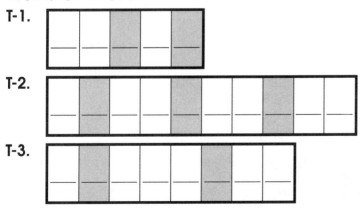

T-1.

T-2.

T-3.

Making and Writing Words Lesson
Challenge Word: periscope

vowels e, e, i, o	consonants c, p, p, r, s

Making Words

	Words	Sentence Clue
1.	crop	The farmer will harvest his crop this fall.
2.	scope	The scope of the film was the entire twentieth century.
3.	spice	Mom always adds a special spice to her sugar cookies.
4.	pipes	The house flooded when the water pipes froze and burst.
5.	prices	Dad says toy prices have gone up since he was a kid.
6.	creeps	It is interesting to see how a lion creeps up on its prey.
7.	piece	I had a piece of chocolate cake for dessert.
8.	pierce	Did it hurt to pierce your ears?
9.	corps	The corps of cadets marched across the parade ground.
10.	copies	I gave copies of my report to all of my classmates.
11.	recipes	Mom has several different recipes for baking bread.
12.	precise	The clock in our classroom keeps very precise time.
13.	copier	I made copies of the letter on the copier in Dad's office.
14.	copper	Pennies are made of copper mixed with other metals.
15.	periscope	

Sorts:
words containing consonant blends; words containing "s" sounds; words relating to food; words that are plural

Transfer Words

	Words	Clue
1.	telescope	Mike uses his telescope to look at the stars.
2.	piercing	The cat made a piercing scream last night.
3.	precision	Surgeons must operate with great care and precision.

Name _____

Making and Writing Words Worksheet

vowels	consonants

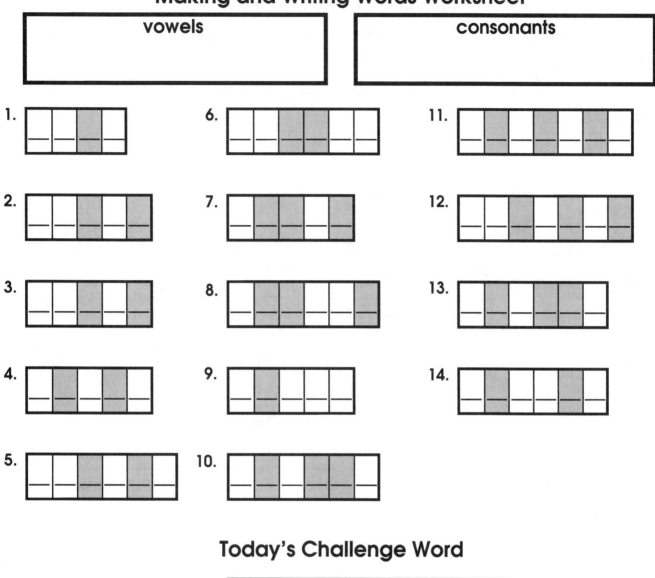

1.
2.
3.
4.
5.
6.
7.
8.
9.
10.
11.
12.
13.
14.

Today's Challenge Word

15.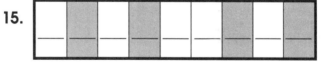

Transfer Words

T-1.
T-2.
T-3.

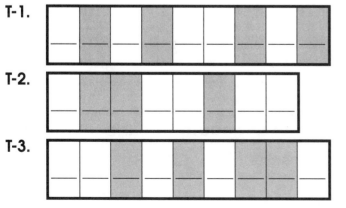

Making and Writing Words Lesson

Challenge Word: residence

vowels	consonants
e, e, e, i	**c, d, n, r, s**

Making Words

	Words	Sentence Clue
1.	rinse	Before I eat the apple, I will rinse it with water.
2.	dense	The dense fog made it difficult to see.
3.	since	Since I am finished with my homework, I can play now.
4.	siren	I heard the siren wail as the fire trucks rushed by.
5.	side	One side of the piece of paper has been colored red.
6.	reside	I reside in a two-story house with a front porch.
7.	sneer	Some people might sneer if they don't like what you say.
8.	sender	The post office stamped the letter "Return to sender."
9.	sneered	My brother sneered when Dad said he was grounded.
10.	sincere	I am sincere when I say that I like you very much.
11.	needier	The victims of the earthquake are needier than we are.
12.	discern	Were you able to discern the date on that old coin?
13.	cinders	Only burnt cinders were left in the fireplace by morning.
14.	screened	Our screened porch was the perfect place to have dinner.
15.	residence	

Sorts:

words containing long "e" sounds; words containing "in" sounds; words that have words within them

Transfer Words

	Words	Clue
1.	needy	We took up a collection for the needy in our community.
2.	sincerity	I was impressed with the sincerity of the mayor.
3.	sneering	The crowd was sneering as the politician talked.

Name _____

Making and Writing Words Worksheet

vowels	consonants

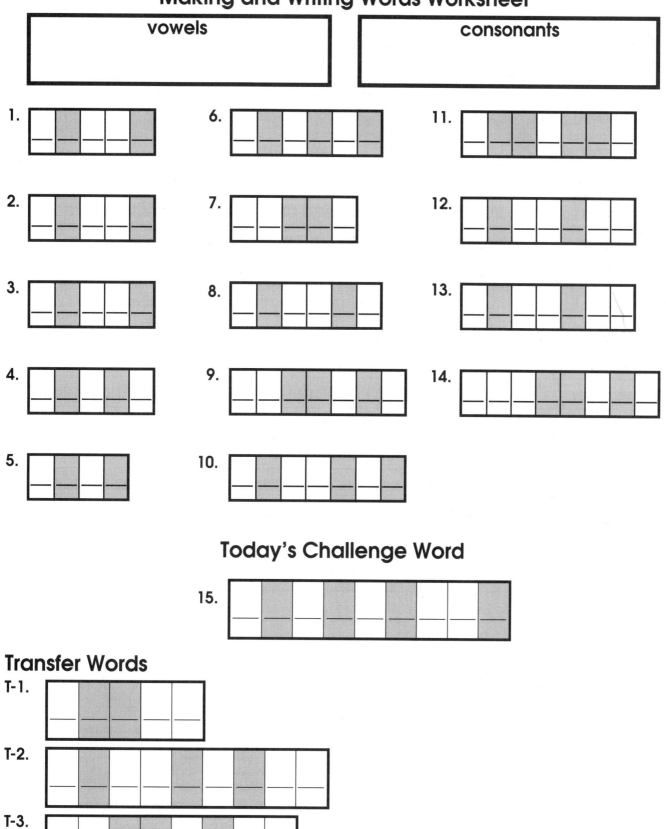

1.

2.

3.

4.

5.

6.

7.

8.

9.

10.

11.

12.

13.

14.

Today's Challenge Word

15.

Transfer Words

T-1.

T-2.

T-3.

137

Making and Writing Words Lesson
Challenge Word: spectator

vowels	consonants
a, e, o	**c, p, r, s, t, t**

Making Words

	Words	Sentence Clue
1.	trace	I like to trace interesting pictures from magazines.
2.	rotate	Volleyball players often rotate positions during a match.
3.	captor	The captor released the hostages after three days.
4.	carpet	We have a soft carpet in our living room.
5.	teapot	Mom took the whistling teapot off the stove.
6.	potter	The potter made several kinds of cups and bowls today.
7.	spotter	The coach asked me to be a spotter for the gymnasts.
8.	toaster	Every morning, I put bread in the toaster to make toast.
9.	coaster	I would love to ride on a roller coaster.
10.	seaport	New York is a large seaport on the Atlantic coast.
11.	scatter	My dad will scatter grass seed on the lawn tomorrow.
12.	protect	Parents need to love and protect their children.
13.	protest	People marched and carried signs to protest the war.
14.	precast	The concrete slabs were precast at the factory.
15.	spectator	

Sorts:
1, 2, and 3 syllable words; words containing "er" sounds; words that have words within them

Transfer Words

	Words	Clue
1.	protection	When rollerblading, I wear a helmet for protection.
2.	rotation	The earth makes one rotation every twenty-four hours.
3.	capture	The enemy came up with a plan to capture our leaders.

Name _____

Making and Writing Words Worksheet

vowels	consonants

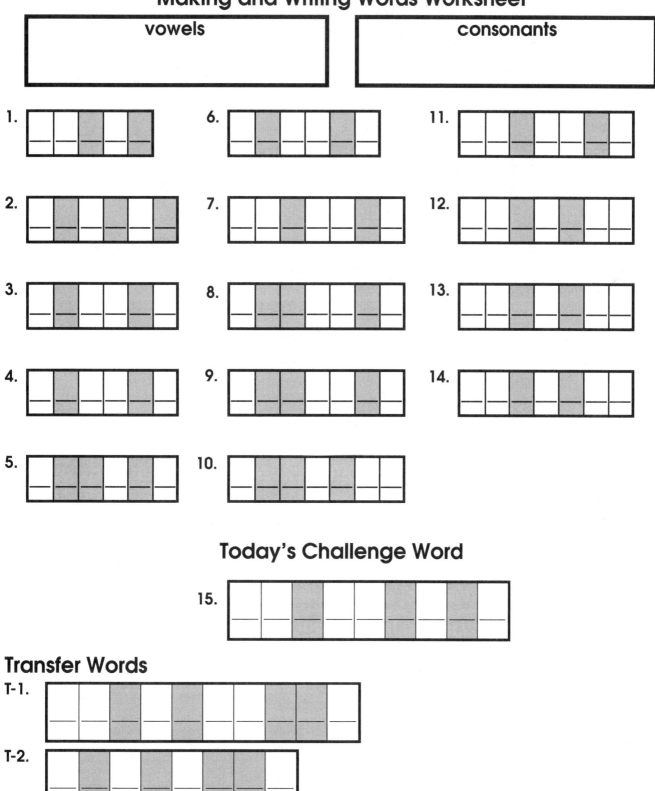

1.

2.

3.

4.

5.

6.

7.

8.

9.

10.

11.

12.

13.

14.

Today's Challenge Word

15.

Transfer Words

T-1.

T-2.

T-3.

Making and Writing Words Lesson
Challenge Word: temporary

vowels	consonants
a, e, o	**m, p, r, r, t, y***

Making Words

	Words	Sentence Clue
1.	roam	I would love to roam the country taking pictures.
2.	tray	The waiter carried our food out on a tray.
3.	tremor	The tremor from the earthquake shook my house.
4.	tamper	Do not tamper with the lock on the safe.
5.	rotary	An airplane propeller moves in a rotary motion.
6.	report	He did a lot of research on Africa for his report.
7.	prayer	I said a prayer that we would win the championship.
8.	porter	Give your bags to the porter when you get on the train.
9.	poetry	I love the way words flow and rhyme in poetry.
10.	parrot	Tina's pet parrot has brightly colored feathers.
11.	martyr	Joan of Arc is a famous martyr who died for her beliefs.
12.	artery	An artery is an important blood vessel.
13.	armory	The soldiers met at the armory to practice marching.
14.	portray	The actor tried to portray sadness through his tears.
15.	temporary	

Sorts:
words containing "er" sounds; words containing long "a" sounds; words that have words within them

Transfer Words

	Words	Clue
1.	temper	I try not to lose my temper even when I am angry.
2.	tantrum	The child threw a tantrum because he was feeling sick.
3.	portrait	The artist painted a portrait of my family.

Name _____

Making and Writing Words Worksheet

vowels	consonants

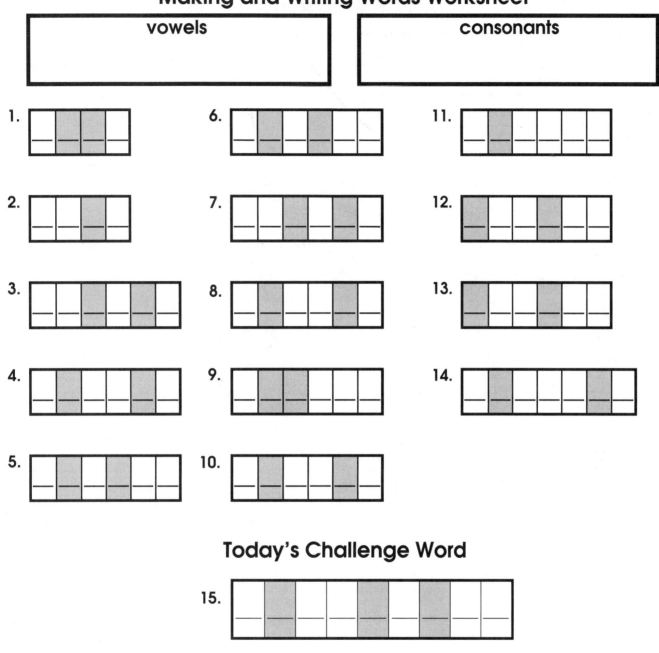

1.
2.
3.
4.
5.
6.
7.
8.
9.
10.
11.
12.
13.
14.

Today's Challenge Word

15.

Transfer Words

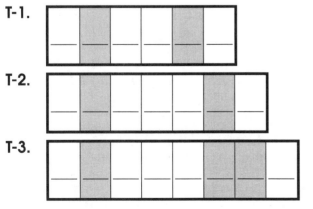

T-1.

T-2.

T-3.

Making and Writing Words Lesson
Challenge Word: confidence

vowels	consonants
e, e, i, o	**c, c, d, f, n, n**

Making Words

Words	Sentence Clue
1. coin	I tossed a coin into the fountain for good luck.
2. cone	I ordered a scoop of vanilla ice cream in a sugar cone.
3. code	Only those who knew the code could read the message.
4. nice	That nice little boy shared all of his toys with us.
5. niece	Aunt Pam says that I am her favorite niece.
6. fined	Judy was fined ten dollars for parking illegally.
7. fiend	The fiend terrorized the city with his criminal actions.
8. fence	We built a wooden fence around the backyard for our dog.
9. define	She looked in the dictionary in order to define the word.
10. conned	I was conned out of fifty dollars by the crook.
11. confine	The warden will confine the prisoners to their cells.
12. confide	Julia's best friend is the only person she can confide in.
13. concede	We finally had to concede that we lost the game.
14. confined	The prisoner was confined to his jail cell.
15. confidence	

Sorts:

1, 2, and 3+ syllable words; words containing long vowel sounds; words containing vowel digraphs; words that have words within them

Transfer Words

Words	Clue
1. friendly	The friendly dog greets everyone in the neighborhood.
2. definition	You can find the definition of a word in the dictionary.
3. concession	We went to the concession stand for hot dogs and drinks.

Name _____

Making and Writing Words Worksheet

vowels	consonants

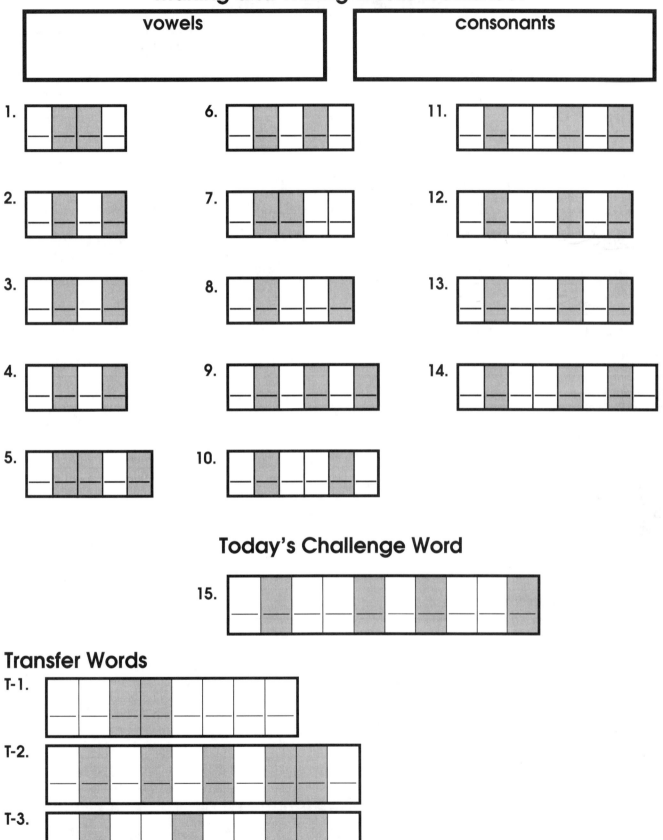

1.

2.

3.

4.

5.

6.

7.

8.

9.

10.

11.

12.

13.

14.

Today's Challenge Word

15.

Transfer Words

T-1.

T-2.

T-3.

Making and Writing Words Lesson
Challenge Word: experiment

vowels	consonants
e, e, e, i	**m, n, p, r, t, x**

Making Words

	Words	Sentence Clue
1.	pint	I bought a pint of milk at the grocery store.
2.	mint	This breath mint has a strong but pleasant taste.
3.	print	We learn to print before we learn to write in cursive.
4.	prime	My dad says that he is in the prime of his life.
5.	temper	The little boy lost his temper when his brother took his toy.
6.	repent	The judge told the criminal to repent his unlawful ways.
7.	permit	I hope my parents will permit me to go to the party.
8.	expire	This coupon will expire at the end of the month.
9.	expert	The expert taught the students how to rock climb.
10.	exempt	First graders are exempt from taking the science test.
11.	entree	I ordered an appetizer and an entree at the restaurant.
12.	entire	The entire class got A's on the math test.
13.	empire	The British empire once stretched around the world.
14.	extreme	The extreme cold made it dangerous to go outside.
15.	experiment	

Sorts:

1, 2, and 3+ syllable words; words containing short "i" sounds; words containing long "i" sounds; words that have words within them

Transfer Words

	Words	Clue
1.	printer	I hope we buy a color printer for our computer.
2.	expiration	The expiration date on the milk carton read March 6th.
3.	exemption	The colonists received an exemption from the new taxes.

Name _____

Making and Writing Words Worksheet

vowels	consonants

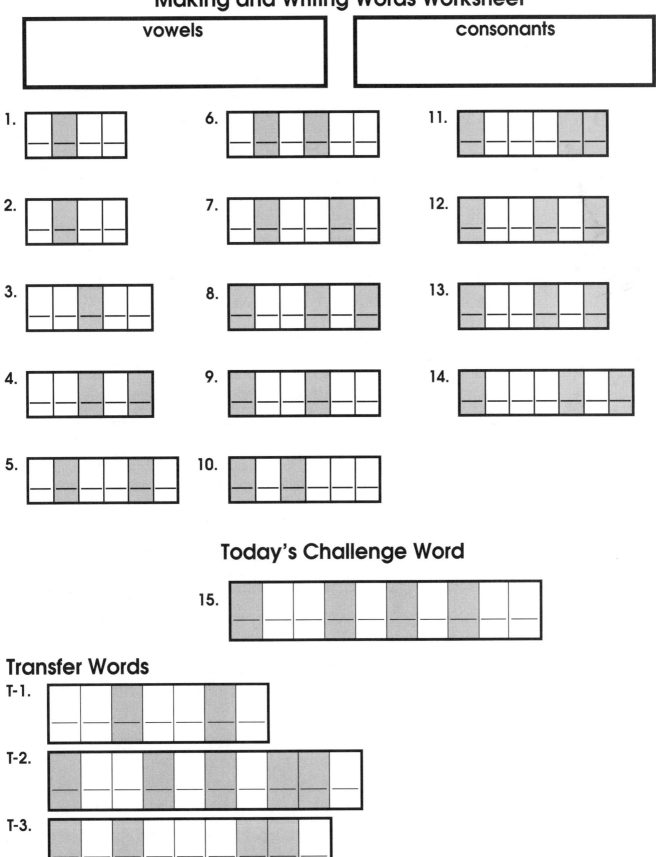

1.

2.

3.

4.

5.

6.

7.

8.

9.

10.

11.

12.

13.

14.

Today's Challenge Word

15.

Transfer Words

T-1.

T-2.

T-3.

Making and Writing Words Lesson
Challenge Word: impossible

vowels	consonants
e, i, i, o	**b, l, m, p, s, s**

Making Words

	Words	Sentence Clue
1.	bliss	The newlyweds were in a state of constant bliss.
2.	spoils	Grandmother always spoils us with candy and toys.
3.	smiles	That boy always smiles when he is happy.
4.	slopes	Those snowy slopes look perfect for downhill skiing.
5.	simple	I thought the math problem was very simple.
6.	posies	Flowers are sometimes referred to as posies.
7.	poise	The young girl acted with poise and grace.
8.	blimps	I saw three blimps moving through the cloudless sky.
9.	simile	A simile is a comparison using the words "like" or "as."
10.	mobile	The musical mobile hung over the baby's crib.
11.	impose	The government plans to impose a new tax on gasoline.
12.	possible	It is possible that our candidate will win the election.
13.	missile	The Air Force plans to test a new missile this afternoon.
14.	implies	Nodding your head implies that you agree with me.
15.	impossible	

Sorts:

1, 2, and 3+ syllable words; words containing diphthongs; words that have words within them; words referring to things that travel through the air

Transfer Words

	Words	Clue
1.	simplest	I try to find the simplest solution to any problem.
2.	mobility	The crutches gave the injured man added mobility.
3.	impossibility	Seeing snow in July in Florida is a near impossibility.

Name _____

Making and Writing Words Worksheet

vowels	consonants

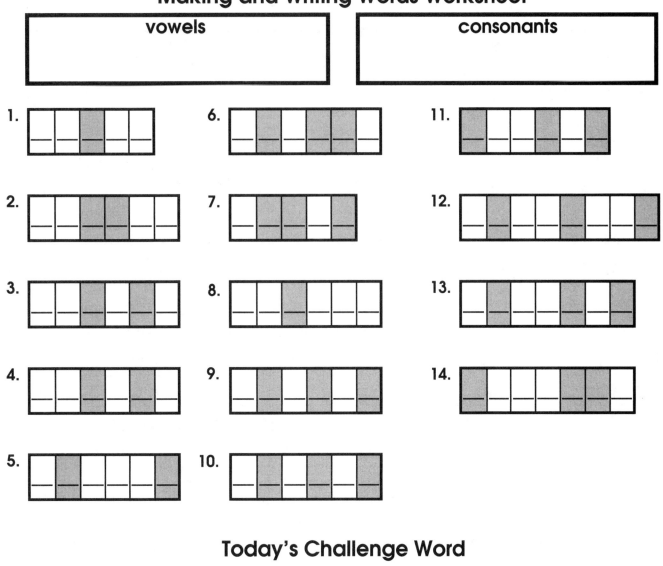

1.

2.

3.

4.

5.

6.

7.

8.

9.

10.

11.

12.

13.

14.

Today's Challenge Word

15.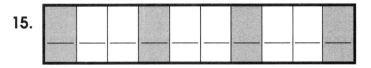

Transfer Words

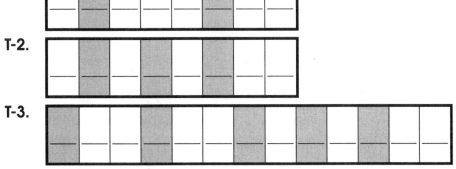

T-1.

T-2.

T-3.

Making and Writing Words Lesson
Challenge Word: starvation

vowels	consonants
a, a, i, o	**n, r, s, t, t, v**

Making Words

Words	Sentence Clue
1. stint	My older brother had a stint in the armed forces.
2. titans	Thomas Edison was one of the titans of invention.
3. strait	Our small boat passed through the narrow strait easily.
4. strain	The argument put a strain on our friendship.
5. sonata	Freddie played a beautiful sonata on the piano.
6. savior	Our team needed a savior to win the game.
7. ratio	I compared the ratio of teachers to students in the class.
8. attain	You can attain your goals in life if you are willing to work.
9. ration	Joe tried to ration his candy to make it last three weeks.
10. artist	The artist painted a beautiful picture of the flowers.
11. transit	The transit company added six new buses to its fleet.
12. station	We went to the train station to pick up my grandmother.
13. artisan	We bought three paintings from the talented artisan.
14. aviators	The aviators planned to fly their planes at the air show.
15. starvation	

Sorts:

1, 2, and 3+ syllable words; words containing "sh" sounds; words containing long "a" sounds; words referring to people

Transfer Words

Words	Clue
1. straight	The shortest distance between two points is a straight line.
2. rational	Are dogs capable of having rational thoughts?
3. nationality	Those flags signify each team's nationality.

Name _____

Making and Writing Words Worksheet

vowels	consonants

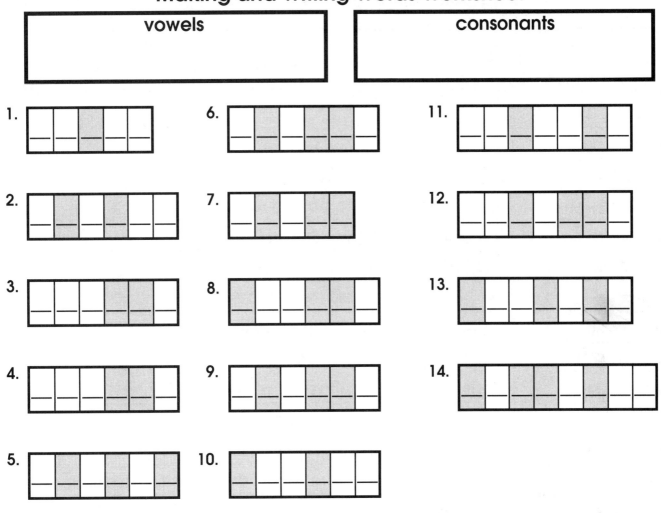

1.
6.
11.

2.
7.
12.

3.
8.
13.

4.
9.
14.

5.
10.

Today's Challenge Word

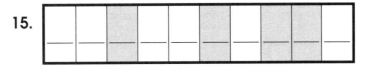

15.

Transfer Words

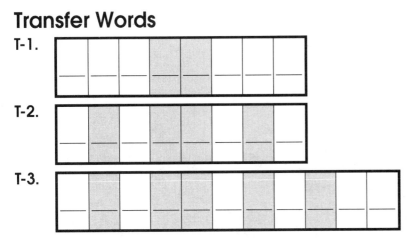

T-1.

T-2.

T-3.

Making and Writing Words Lesson
Challenge Word: suggestion

vowels e, i, o, u	consonants g, g, n, s, s, t

Making Words

	Words	Sentence Clue
1.	gust	The strong gust of wind blew the hat off my head.
2.	guest	Sam invited Jerry to be a guest at his house.
3.	sting	The bee will sting you if you bother it.
4.	stung	Joe yelled out in pain after the bee stung his foot.
5.	sinus	My allergies caused me to have a sinus headache.
6.	tossing	Steve and his dad were outside tossing a baseball.
7.	tongues	We jokingly stuck out our tongues at each other.
8.	ingest	Dogs tend to ingest their food too quickly.
9.	suggest	I suggest you check your answer to that math problem.
10.	outings	While on vacation, we made many outings to the beach.
11.	nuggets	The gold nuggets were found deep within the mine.
12.	noise	The traffic jam created a lot of noise during rush hour.
13.	soggiest	The soggiest piece of bread has the most butter on it.
14.	guessing	We were guessing who the winner of the race would be.
15.	suggestion	

Sorts:
words containing double consonants; words containing "ing" endings; words that are plural; words containing short "u" sounds

Transfer Words

	Words	Clue
1.	soggy	The dog was wet and soggy after playing in the rain.
2.	stinging	My cheeks are still stinging from the icy wind.
3.	noisiest	The crying baby was the noisiest child I'd ever heard.

Name _____

Making and Writing Words Worksheet

vowels	consonants

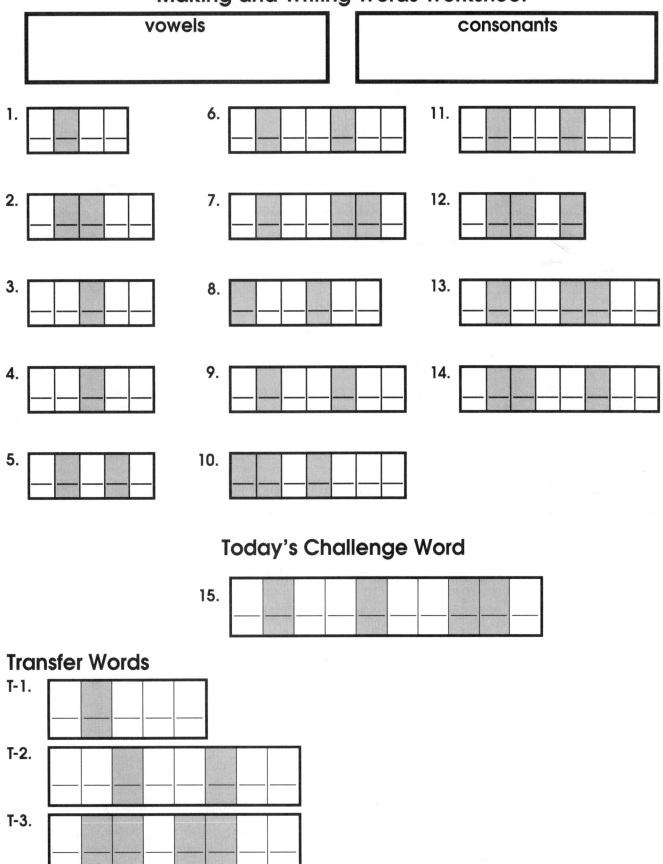

1.

2.

3.

4.

5.

6.

7.

8.

9.

10.

11.

12.

13.

14.

Today's Challenge Word

15.

Transfer Words

T-1.

T-2.

T-3.

Making and Writing Words Lesson
Challenge Word: celebration

vowels	consonants
a, e, e, i, o	**b, c, l, n, r, t**

Making Words

	Words	Sentence Clue
1.	tile	The tile on the kitchen counter was scratched and worn.
2.	late	Were you late for band practice today?
3.	tale	The story of Paul Bunyan is my favorite tall tale.
4.	clean	I did not clean my room, so I cannot play outside.
5.	clear	Every night after dinner, I help my mom clear the table.
6.	coral	My family went snorkeling near a coral reef in Florida.
7.	cereal	I had cereal and fruit for breakfast this morning.
8.	create	It can take a long time to create a work of art.
9.	relate	I can relate to other people who are the same age.
10.	rebate	My parents got a fifty dollar rebate with the new stereo.
11.	bracelet	My favorite bracelet is gold with small silver charms.
12.	oriental	The oriental figurines were carved from jade.
13.	tolerance	He has a low tolerance for pain.
14.	noticeable	The scratch on my arm is barely noticeable.
15.	celebration	

Sorts:

1, 2, and 3+ syllable words; words containing long "a" sounds; words containing "s" sounds; words containing consonant blends; words that have words within them

Transfer Words

	Words	Clue
1.	tolerate	Sammy learned to tolerate his baby brother's crying.
2.	orientation	All college freshmen are expected to attend orientation.
3.	relation	Although our last name is Smith, he is no relation to me.

Name _____

Making and Writing Words Worksheet

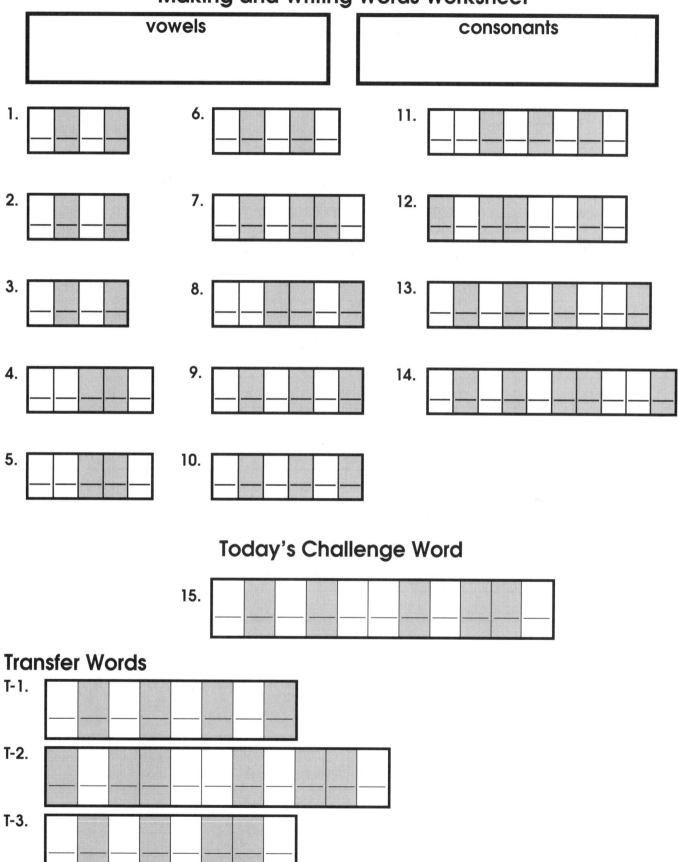

vowels	consonants

1.
2.
3.
4.
5.
6.
7.
8.
9.
10.
11.
12.
13.
14.

Today's Challenge Word

15.

Transfer Words

T-1.
T-2.
T-3.

153

Making and Writing Words Lesson
Challenge Word: independent

vowels	consonants
e, e, e, i	**d, d, n, n, n, p, t**

Making Words

Words	Sentence Clue
1. pinned	I pinned my award ribbons to my jacket.
2. needed	Our team needed a rest after the long run.
3. intend	I intend to go to the movies this afternoon.
4. indeed	Our school is indeed a great one!
5. edited	Sammy edited my paper before I turned it in.
6. dieted	I dieted for six weeks and lost ten pounds.
7. depend	We depend on the bus driver to get us to school safely.
8. denied	She denied that she took the candy and ate it.
9. dented	The hailstones dented the hood of the new car.
10. deepen	Your kindness will deepen my fond feelings for you.
11. nineteen	Twelve plus seven equals nineteen.
12. intended	I intended to clean my room, but I never got around to it.
13. dependent	Babies are very dependent on their parents.
14. indented	All the paragraphs in my report were indented perfectly.
15. independent	

Sorts:

1, 2, and 3+ syllable words; words containing long "e" sounds; words containing suffixes or inflected endings; words that have words within them

Transfer Words

Words	Clue
1. intention	Our intention is to surprise Mom by cleaning the house.
2. indentation	Use proper indentation when beginning new paragraphs.
3. edition	I think that the first edition of the book is the best version.

Name _____

Making and Writing Words Worksheet

vowels	consonants

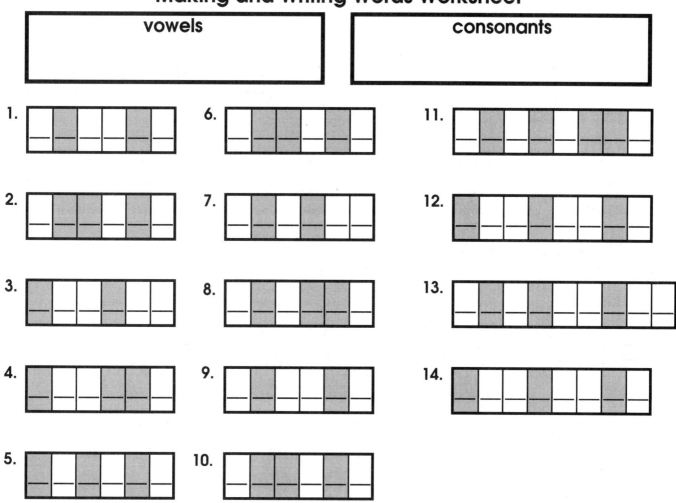

1.
2.
3.
4.
5.
6.
7.
8.
9.
10.
11.
12.
13.
14.

Today's Challenge Word

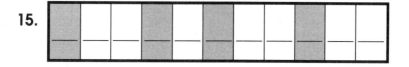

15.

Transfer Words

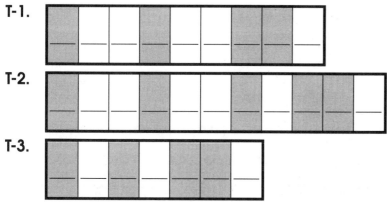

T-1.

T-2.

T-3.

155

Making and Writing Words Lesson
Challenge Word: masterpiece

vowels	consonants
a, e, e, e, i	**c, m, p, r, s, t**

Making Words

	Words	Sentence Clue
1.	crepe	We decorated the room with crepe paper streamers.
2.	creep	The mouse tried to creep past the cat to get the cheese.
3.	piece	I enjoyed a piece of pie for dessert.
4.	price	The price of groceries just keeps going up.
5.	prime	At the steak restaurant, I ordered the prime rib.
6.	cream	The recipe says to mix butter, sugar, and cream.
7.	create	He loves to create silly nicknames for all of his friends.
8.	carpet	The new carpet in my bedroom is pale yellow.
9.	escape	We could not escape the noise from the construction site.
10.	receipts	I made sure to get receipts for all of my purchases.
11.	permeates	The smell of grilled hamburgers permeates the air.
12.	steamier	The mirror got steamier as the shower water got hotter.
13.	peacetime	I prefer peacetime over periods of war.
14.	creamiest	The milkshake was the creamiest I had ever tasted.
15.	masterpiece	

Sorts:

1, 2, and 3 syllable words; words containing "s" sounds; words containing long "e" sounds; words containing vowel digraphs

Transfer Words

	Words	Clue
1.	receive	Did you receive the letter that I sent you last week?
2.	primates	Monkeys, chimps, and gorillas are considered primates.
3.	steamiest	High humidity made this the steamiest day of the summer.

Name _____

Making and Writing Words Worksheet

vowels	consonants

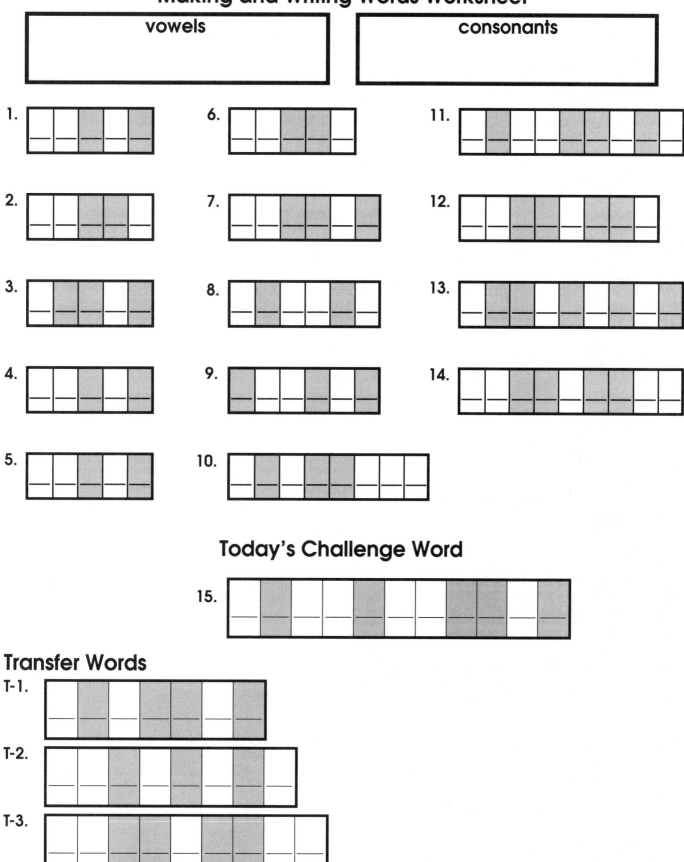

1.
2.
3.
4.
5.
6.
7.
8.
9.
10.
11.
12.
13.
14.

Today's Challenge Word

15.

Transfer Words

T-1.
T-2.
T-3.

References

Cunningham, P. M. & Cunningham, J. W. (1992). "Making Words: Enhancing the Invented Spelling-Decoding Connection." *The Reading Teacher*, 46, pp.106-115.

Cunningham, P. M., Hall, D. P., & Defee, M. (1991). "Non-ability Grouped, Multilevel Instruction: A Year in a First Grade Classroom." *The Reading Teacher*, 44, pp. 566-571.

Cunningham, P. M., Hall, D. P., & Defee, M. (1998). "Non-ability Grouped, Multilevel Instruction: Eight Years Later." *The Reading Teacher*, 51, pp. 652-664.

Snow, C. E., Burns, M. S., & Griffin, P. (1998). *Preventing Reading Difficulties in Young Children*. Washington, D.C., National Academy Press.

Stahl, S. A., Duffy-Hester, A. M., & Stahl, K. A. D. (1998). "Everything You Wanted to Know about Phonics (But Were Afraid to Ask)." *Reading Research Quarterly*, 33, pp. 338-355.

Notes

Notes